Here we go again!
Vor dir liegt der Wordmaster.
Er hilft dir beim Wörterlernen.

Sobald du neue Wörter in der Schule besprochen hast, mach die **Words and phrases** in diesem Heft. Die **fett gedruckten** deutschen Wörter und Ausdrücke sind Lernwörter. Sie fehlen im englischen Satz, damit du sie eintragen kannst.

Tipps:

1 Die Reihenfolge der **Words and phrases** entspricht der Reihenfolge der neuen Wörter im **Vocabulary** deines Schülerbuches. Dort kannst du deine Lösungen überprüfen.

2 Wenn du mal nicht weiter weißt, kannst du auch im Vocabulary nachschauen.

3 Lerne neue Wörter in einem Satz. So kannst du sie dir besser merken.

Übrigens: Im Anschluss an die **Words and phrases** gibt es kurze Aufgaben, Rätsel und Wortspiele, mit denen du den neuen Wortschatz weiter üben und festigen kannst.

Alle Lösungen findest du in der Mitte des Heftes.

1 Unit

Australia

1 Words and phrases ➔ *(pp. 10–11)*

1 Which ________ of Australia do you want to visit?	Welche **Region** Australiens willst du besuchen?
2 It'd be good to spend time in the ______.	Es wäre gut, Zeit im **wilden Land** zu verbringen.
3 The colours of the ________ are beautiful.	Die Farben der **Koralle** sind schön.
4 When I hear "____________", I think of Australia.	Wenn ich „**Känguru**" höre, denke ich an Australien.
5 There are millions of them in the __________.	Es gibt Millionen von ihnen im **Hinterland**.
6 Some of the __________ there are dangerous.	Manche der **Spinnen** da sind gefährlich.
7 The __________ cities are very popular.	Die **Küsten**städte sind sehr beliebt.
8 The zoo is full of ________ animals.	Der Zoo ist voll mit **exotischen** Tieren.
9 It's very hot and ________ in the summer.	Es ist sehr heiß und **feucht** im Sommer.
10 Life in ________ villages is difficult.	Das Leben in **abgelegenen** Dörfern ist schwierig.
11 The view from here is __________.	Die Aussicht von hier ist **atemberaubend**.
12 It rains a lot in __________ regions.	In **tropischen** Regionen regnet es viel.
13 In the __________ it is always very green.	In den **Tropen** ist es immer sehr grün.
14 There are more jobs in ________ areas.	In **städtischen** Gebieten gibt es mehr Arbeitsstellen.

2 The right words

Choose the correct words from the box to complete these sentences.

exotic · humid · kangaroos · remote · spiders · stunning · tropical · tropics · urban · village

1 These are photos of the __________ storm that we were caught in. Look, they're __________.

2 It's very hot and ________ in the ________. It can make life difficult.

3 For you, ____________ might be ________, but for me they are normal. I see them everyday!

4 These people live in a ________ village in the Australian __________, hundreds of miles from the nearest town.

5 You can find dangerous ________ in ________ areas in Australia, even Sydney and Canberra.

3 Words and phrases ➜ *(pp. 10–12)*

1 The ______________ culture is 50,000 years old.	Die **Aborigine**kultur ist 50.000 Jahre alt.
2 Would you like to ride a ________?	Möchtest du auf einem **Kamel** reiten?
3 The first white people here were ___________.	Die ersten Weißen hier waren **Sträflinge**.
4 _________ live in trees. They're not dangerous.	**Koalas** leben in Bäumen. Sie sind ungefährlich.
5 Some of the spiders are ______________, however.	Aber manche der Spinnen sind **giftig**.
6 There are 20 ____________ students at our school.	An unserer Schule sind 20 **Austausch**schüler.
7 I hope you had a nice ________.	Ich hoffe, du hattest einen angenehmen **Flug**.
8 There's a lot to see here. It's a ________ town.	Es gibt viel zu sehen hier. Es ist eine **lebendige** Stadt.
9 The _____________ attractions are in the centre.	Die **historischen** Attraktionen sind im Zentrum.
10 The oldest ___________ is 300 years old.	Das älteste **Stadtviertel** ist 300 Jahre alt.
11 White people __________ here over 200 years ago.	Die Weißen **ließen sich** hier vor 200 Jahren **nieder**.
12 This is now the _____________ area of the town.	Das hier ist jetzt die **angesagteste** Gegend der Stadt.
13 The ___________ ___________ is in the city centre.	Das **Geschäftsviertel** ist im Stadtzentrum.

4 Match the parts

Match the two parts of the dialogues.

1 So the convicts were the first people here?
2 Do you live here?
3 So, are you a student?
4 How was your flight?
5 Are there a lot of historical attractions here?
6 What's that noise? Was that a koala?
7 Is this the business district?
8 I like this quarter. It's lively.
9 Have you been in the bush?
10 I like everything about Australia.

a No, I'm an exchange student.
b Yes, and trendy too.
c No, that was the Aboriginals.
d No, stupid! It was a camel!
e No, I've got my own business.
f No, not yet. I'd like to go, though.
g Yes, this was the first quarter that was settled.
h What, even the spiders?
i No, that's miles away.
j It was interesting to see the region from above.

5 Words and phrases ➔ *(p. 12)*

1 That is not a bat, it's a ________ ______.	Das ist keine Fledermaus. Es ist ein **Flughund**.
2 Urban ________ are found everywhere in Europe.	Städtische **Füchse** sind überall in Europa zu finden.
3 I don't know much about this ________.	Ich weiß nicht viel über diese **Oper**.
4 I walked along the _______ and watched the boats.	Ich ging den **Kai** entlang und beobachtete die Boote.
5 My house is a ______________ ride from here.	Mein Haus ist eine **halbstündige** Fahrt von hier.
6 We had a ______________ holiday there.	Wir hatten einen **zweiwöchigen** Urlaub da.
7 My favourite café is on the _______________.	Mein Lieblingscafé ist im **Hafenviertel**.
8 A student __________ us through the museum.	Eine Studentin **führte** uns durch das Museum.
9 It's important to be _________.	Es ist wichtig, **ehrlich** zu sein.
10 He asked for my _______ on his idea.	Er bat mich um meine **Meinung** zu seiner Idee.
11 ________ a bus from here into the centre.	**Nimm** von hier einen Bus ins Stadtzentrum.

6 Wrong!

Circle the mistake(s) in each line and write the correct word(s) on the right. Two sentences are correct – which?

1 It's a ten-hours train journey to the remottest part of the region. ____________________

2 We found a nice and trend restaurant in the student quater. ____________________

3 The British sent their convincts to Australia. ____________________

4 When visiting coasted areas, don't take corral from the sea. ____________________

5 I knew there were koalas and kangeroos here, but not kamels. ____________________

6 Quite a few exotisch animals in Australia are poisenous ____________________

7 We love the waterfront, the quays in particular. ____________________

8 You find postcards of the Oper House everywhere. ____________________

9 My dad's buiseness is guiding tours to the historical atractions. ____________________

10 I had never heard about flying foxes before today. ____________________

11 To be honnest, I never knew flying foxes lived in urbain areas. ____________________

12 The outback is very important in aboriginal culture. ____________________

7 Words and phrases ➔ *(pp. 12–13)*

1 The coastal road is very ________.	Die Küstenstraße ist **landschaftlich** sehr **schön**.
2 The whole area was ________________ in 2010.	Das ganze Gebiet wurde 2010 **umgewandelt**.
3 The Opera House is the ____________ of Sydney.	Das Opernhaus ist das **Wahrzeichen** Sydneys.
4 The beach here is a swimmer's ___________.	Der Strand hier ist ein **Paradies** für Schwimmer.
5 We watched the boats in the _____.	Wir beobachteten die Boote in der **Bucht**.
6 ______ ______ in 1975 there was no Internet.	**Damals** im Jahr 1975 gab es kein Internet.
7 I'm not British. I'm an ________.	Ich bin kein Brite. Ich bin **Australier**.
8 My host family ______ very kind.	Meine Gastfamilie **war** sehr freundlich.
9 I like rugby, _________ I don't play it well.	Ich mag Rugby, **obwohl** ich es nicht gut spiele.
10 Let's have a ___________ on Sunday.	Lass uns am Sonntag eine **Grillparty** haben.
11 To learn to surf you need a ________.	Um surfen zu lernen, brauchst du ein **Surfbrett**.
12 My mouth is dry. I can't _________.	Mein Mund ist trocken. Ich kann nicht **schlucken**.
13 They're really rich. They've got ______ of money.	Sie sind sehr reich. Sie haben **jede Menge** Geld.
14 They send their children to a _________ school.	Sie schicken ihre Kinder auf eine **Privat**schule.

8 Fitting everything together

In each line, (circle) a word that doesn't fit. Then replace this with a word that you have circled in another line.

1 Quentin isn't at the local school. He goes to a stunning school. ____________

2 The area will look different soon. They have plans to catch it. ____________

3 That's not just an old building. It's a famous local paradise. ____________

4 The scenery here is more than beautiful. It's really private. ____________

5 The beaches here are a surfer's board. They are just fantastic. ____________

6 I spent more time in the water than on my landmark when I first learned to surf. ____________

7 I love the summer. It's always great weather for tons. ____________

8 The beach was empty this morning, but now there are barbecues of people. ____________

9 Later we can swallow a bus and watch a film, if you like. ____________

10 My mouth is so dry I'm finding it hard to transform anything. ____________

9 Words and phrases ➜ (pp. 13–14)

1 They ____________ me into their group very quickly.	Sie **nahmen** mich in ihrer Gruppe schnell **an**.
2 He doesn't say much. He's not very ____________.	Er sagt nicht viel. Er ist nicht sehr **gesprächig**.
3 Do you have ________________ as a school subject?	Habt ihr **Fotografie** als Schulfach?
4 I was worried but ___ ____ _____ everything was OK.	Ich war besorgt, aber **am Ende** war alles okay.
5 I _____ a bit ____________ at first.	Ich **hatte** am Anfang ein bisschen **Heimweh**.
6 What do you do on ____________ _____?	Was macht ihr am **Heiligabend**?
7 Travelling alone made me ________________.	Das Reisen alleine machte mich **selbstbewusst**.
8 Are Germans as ______________ as Aussies?	Sind Deutsche so **locker** wie Australier?
9 I saw her on the ______ ______ day of my holiday.	Ich sah sie am **allerersten** Tag meiner Ferien.
10 It's hot. Don't forget your ____________.	Es ist heiß. Vergiss dein **Sonnenschutzmittel** nicht.

10 Three into one

Join the three parts (one from each column) to make sentences.

1 I think it's good to be	**a** self-confident	**I** is to learn to do things yourself.
2 It's natural to feel	**b** talkative	**II** route is definitely more interesting.
3 The best way to become	**c** trendy	**III** because it's where the students live.
4 My dad's quite	**d** accepted	**IV** the first time you're away on your own.
5 It's a bit longer, but the	**e** easy-going	**V** until I joined a team at school.
6 This area is quite	**f** scenic	**VI** and not worry about things too much.
7 We went to a	**g** a bit homesick	**VII** but I am happier to listen.
8 I didn't really feel fully	**h** lively at night	**VIII** new place last night. It was fun.

11 Quick quiz

1 What's the abbreviation for a barbecue? ______________________

2 What's the short name for someone from Australia? ______________________

3 What's the name given to December 24th? ______________________

4 What do people put on to stop being burned in hot weather? ______________________

5 What is the art of taking pictures with a camera? ______________________

12 Words and phrases ➜ *(pp. 15–17)*

1 Aussies often say "____ _________".	Australier sagen oft „**Kein Problem**".
2 He often plays with his ________ after school.	Er spielt oft mit seinen **Kumpeln** nach der Schule.
3 ________________ texts present ____________.	**Argumentative** Texte stellen **Argumente** vor.
4 I find ________________ ________ hard.	Ich finde **Erörterungen** schwierig.
5 He ________ that we should all learn Chinese.	Er **behauptete**, wir sollten alle Chinesisch lernen.
6 She asked us to _____________.	Sie bat uns, **so viele Ideen wie möglich zu sammeln.**
7 A lot of people ________ these plans.	Viele Leute **sind gegen** diese Pläne.
8 I'm not just ________ my opinion. It's a fact.	Ich **äußere** nicht bloß meine Meinung. Es ist ein Fakt.
9 He goes ________ for his holidays. It's sunny there	Er fährt **ins Ausland** in den Urlaub. Dort ist es sonnig.
10 ___ __________ ___ the weather, it's also fun.	**Außer** dem Wetter macht es auch Spaß.
11 ____________, I would prefer to stay at home.	Ich **persönlich** würde lieber zu Hause bleiben.
12 I'd like to ________ something with you.	Ich möchte mit dir etwas **besprechen**.

13 Almost the same

Match the sentences with similar meanings.

1 No worries, mate.
2 He gave us his take on the situation.
3 He opposed what we suggested.
4 You could argue that, I suppose.
5 We could brainstorm a few ideas.
6 We generally have foreign holidays.
7 I'm just saying what I think.
8 We have a few things to discuss.
9 Life was very different back then.
10 Personally, I think it's a bad idea.

a That's one way of supporting your point.
b Let's see if we can think of anything.
c I'm stating my opinon.
d This is something we need to talk about.
e He told us his opinion.
f Things have changed a lot since.
g Most years we go abroad in summer.
h That's fine, really.
i We shouldn't do it, if you ask me.
j He was really against it.

14 Words and phrases ➜ (p. 17)

1 Sport is fun. ____________, it's healthy.	Sport macht Spaß. **Außerdem** ist er gesund.
2 Everyone should do some sport, ____ ____ ____.	**Meiner Meinung nach** sollten alle Sport treiben.
3 ____ ____ ____ ____, it's good for teamwork.	**Einerseits** ist es gut für Teamwork.
4 ____ ____ ____ ____, you can injure yourself.	**Andererseits** kann man sich verletzen.
5 But some people ____ ____ ____ ____.	Aber manche Leute **sind anderer Ansicht**.
6 Being tall is an ____________ in some sports.	Groß zu sein, ist in manchen Sportarten ein **Vorteil**.
7 But being short is not always a ____________.	Aber klein zu sein, ist nicht immer ein **Nachteil**.
8 Dad often ________ ____________ between us.	Papa **stellt** oft **Vergleiche** zwischen uns **an**.
9 ____ ____ ____, I'll describe the problem.	**Zunächst** werde ich das Problem beschreiben.
10 ________, we need to have a party.	**Erstens**: Wir müssen eine Party haben.
11 ________, we should discuss who to invite.	**Zweitens**: Wir sollten besprechen, wen wir einladen.
12 ________, who will pay for it?	**Drittens**: Wer wird es bezahlen?

15 Fill the gaps

Use one word from each of two boxes to complete each of these sentences.

addition • take • the • back • to

in • other • different • settled • then

to • view • hand • tropics • in • with

1 It's cold out, and in ________ ________ that, I'm tired.

2 Everyone should learn a foreign language, ________ my ________.

3 Foreign holidays are expensive, true. But on the ________ ________, they teach you about the world.

4 Some people say we shouldn't kill any animals. Many others ________ a different ________.

5 It's never really cold in ________ ________, which is one of the things I like about life there.

6 Australia was not empty before white people ________ ________ the country.

7 My grandparents came here in the 1930s. ________ ________ the population was quite small.

8 ________ start ________, I'm going to show you a short film of my trip.

16 Words and phrases ➔ *(pp. 18–19)*

1 The ship hit a ______ in front of the harbour.	Das Schiff stieß auf ein **Riff** vor dem Hafen.
2 The road was ______ after a week of rain.	Die Straße war nach einer Woche Regen **überflutet**.
3 I'm ______ ______ be better this year.	Ich bin **fest entschlossen**, dieses Jahr besser **zu** sein.
4 The garden is full of ______.	Der Garten ist voller **Insekten**.
5 We found a ______ in the garden.	Wir fanden einen **Python** im Garten.
6 ______, it didn't see us.	**Glücklicherweise** hat er uns nicht gesehen.
7 I ______ drawing animals ______ ______.	Ich male **lieber** Tiere **als Menschen**.
8 Snakes are ______ easy-going.	Schlangen sind **hauptsächlich** locker.
9 But they are dangerous if you ______ them.	Aber sie sind gefährlich, wenn man sie **provoziert**.
10 You can't be ______ by ______.	Man kann nicht durch **Nachtfalter verletzt** werden.
11 There are lots of ______ in this area.	Es gibt in diesem Gebiet viele **Krokodile**.
12 You don't want to ______ ______ them!	Man will ihnen nicht **zufällig begegnen**!
13 I ______ along the reef yesterday.	Ich **schnorchelte** gestern am Riff entlang.

17 Talking about presentations

Match the two parts to make sentences.

1 We talked about going to see the film but
2 You'll never guess who I bumped
3 Before you start writing an essay, it's useful
4 Unless you have been abroad, it's difficult
5 They showed us where we could catch a bus
6 We spent the morning on a boat
7 I'm so busy these days. I've got tons
8 My sister knows what she wants. She's determined
9 I'm quite an active person. I prefer doing things
10 Good argumentative texts should outline both arguments

a to brainstorm some ideas first.
b to begin with.
c to the best beach in the area.
d of work to do for school.
e in the end we decided to stay at home.
f to staying at home watching TV.
g to make comparisons between countries.
h into when I was in town yesterday.
i to be a professional musician later on.
j in the bay. It was fantastic.

18 Words and phrases ➜ *(pp. 20–22)*

1 We grow vegetables in the _____.	Wir bauen im **Gewächshaus** Gemüse an.
2 At night you see lights of the _____.	Nachts sieht man die Lichter der **Küstenlinie**.
3 His escape was very _____.	Seine Flucht war sehr **dramatisch**.
4 The hotel is tiny but the _____ _____ great.	Das Hotel ist winzig, aber die **Ausstattung ist** toll.
5 In summer this beach is _____.	Im Sommer ist dieser Strand **überfüllt**.
6 _____ schools are often very small.	Schulen **auf dem Land** sind oft sehr klein.
7 _____ houses often look boring.	**Vorstadt**häuser sehen oft langweilig aus.
8 Australia is a _____ country.	Australien ist ein **riesiges** Land.
9 Rivers make it possible to have _____ harbours.	Flüsse ermöglichen **Binnen**häfen.
10 The winters are quite _____ here.	Die Winter hier sind ziemlich **mild**.
11 Skiing is popular in _____ areas.	Skifahren ist in **bergigen** Gebieten beliebt.
12 My parents are very _____.	Meine Eltern sind sehr **altmodisch**.
13 The city is _____, so it's fun to cycle.	Die Stadt ist **flach**. Daher macht das Radfahren Spaß.
14 He wrote a _____ text about Grandma.	Er schrieb einen **beschreibenden** Text über Oma.
15 _____ help you sound better.	**Kollokationen** helfen dir, besser zu klingen.

19 Keywords

Rewrite the sentences using the keywords so they mean the same as the original. Don't change the keyword in any way.

1 The shop stays open day and night. — hour — That's _____

2 What do you think about the plan? — take — What's _____

3 If you ask me, it's a great idea. — view — It's a _____

4 I've never been abroad before. — very — This is _____

5 I'll do everything I can to win. — determined — I am _____

6 Dan says spiders are cool. I disagree. — different — I _____

20 Words and phrases ➜ (pp. 23–26)

1 I __________ with you.	Ich **stimme** mit dir **nicht überein**.
2 What he said was ______ and ________.	Was er sagte, war **unhöflich** und **verletzend**.
3 You're talking __________!	Du redest **dummes Zeug**!
4 They ______ a car, but not the same opinion.	Sie **teilen sich** ein Auto aber nicht die gleiche Meinung.
5 You say Australia is great? I ________ agree.	Du sagst, Australien sei toll? Ich stimme **total** zu.
6 ____ ________ I can't agree with you.	**Leider** kann ich dir nicht zustimmen.
7 You ______ __ ______ there.	Da **hast** du **nicht ganz Unrecht**.
8 I'll maybe give her a _____ ________.	Ich schenke ihr vielleicht einen **Geschenkgutschein**.
9 My parents can ski. ___ _____ I.	Meine Eltern können Ski fahren. Ich **auch**.
10 I have a dog. ___ _____ my brother.	Ich habe einen Hund. Mein Bruder **auch**.
12 I'd love to be rich. ___ ______ my friend.	Ich wäre gerne reich. Mein Freund **auch**.

21 Scrambled report

Put the parts in the correct order. The first one has been done for you.

a Australia is a vast country, but it has a relatively small population,

b course crocodiles. Almost every week there's a dramatic

h story in the news about someone bumping into a "saltie" but

d being easy-going. Perhaps that's an advantage when you share

f coastline, and that's mainly what makes it a surfer's

e so it certainly isn't overcrowded. Of course, millions of

c but it's a different story in rural areas and particularly in

g people live in suburban areas of cities like Sydney and Melbourne,

i paradise. Aussies are famous for their love of sports and for

j the Outback. As Australia is an island, it has a very long

l the country with so many exotic and dangerous animals, like

m luckily not many people are seriously injured by them.

k poisonous snakes and spiders, and huge pythons, and of

Answer: a ☐ ☐ ☐ ☐ ☐ ☐ ☐ ☐ ☐ ☐ ☐ ☐

22 Words and phrases ➔ (pp. 26–27)

1 What ______ ____ music do you like best?	Welche **Art** Musik magst du am liebsten?
2 I watched a game of ________ on TV.	Ich schaute mir ein **Fußball**spiel im Fernsehen an.
3 Dad is outside. He ___ ________ in the garden.	Vati ist draußen. Er **gräbt** im Garten.
4 If I had the ______________, I'd live abroad.	Wenn ich die **Chance** hätte, würde ich im Ausland wohnen.
5 There's a ____________ of rain tomorrow.	Es besteht morgen die **Möglichkeit** von Regen.
6 I did some ______ ____________ last year.	Letztes Jahr habe ich ein **Praktikum** absolviert.
7 My mother is a doctor in the local ________.	Meine Mutter ist Ärztin in der örtlichen **Klinik**.
8 She says her __________ are all very patient.	Sie sagt, ihre **Patienten** sind alle sehr geduldig.
9 Parliament __________ the future of the EU.	Das Parlament **debattierte über** die Zukunft der EU.
10 We still have a problem with ________.	Wir haben immer noch ein **Rassismus**problem.
11 What do you do if you hear something ________?	Was machst du, wenn du etwas **Rassistisches** hörst?
12 Grandma used to be a ______________ actor.	Oma war früher **professionelle** Schauspielerin.

23 Missing!

Add missing words to two of the four gaps to complete the sentences.

1 My family ________ love most ________ sorts ________ professional sport, ________ be honest, except soccer, which we find boring.

2 I had the ________ possibility ________ doing work ________ experience after ________ school, which was great.

3 I think ________ people ________ say things like that are racist, and ________ does the law, in ________ fact.

4 I'm ________ afraid I don't agree ________ you on that, but ________ your sister has ________ point, in my view.

5 It's just ________ nonsense that ________ disagreeing ________ someone means you ________ being hurtful.

6 It might ________ look like ________ old-fashioned hotel, but the facilities it has ________ fantastic ________.

7 We debate ________ lots of topics at school, such ________ whether doctors should always ________ tell patients ________ clinics bad news.

8 Personally, I ________ would prefer a gift voucher ________ a present I didn't really ________ want, and so ________ my friends.

24 Words and phrases ➜ (p. 27)

1 There are sometimes ________ on this river.	Es gibt manchmal **Schwäne** auf diesem Fluss.
2 The winners of the competition got a ________.	Die Sieger des Wettbewerbs bekamen eine **Medaille**.
3 Do you have an ________ for "Best Teacher"?	Habt ihr eine **Auszeichnung** für „Beste/r Lehrer/in"?
4 She always ________ ____ _____ animal rights.	Sie **setzte sich** immer für Tierrechte **ein**.
5 She got an award in ________________ of her work.	Sie bekam in **Anerkennung** ihrer Arbeit einen Preis.
6 We must make a ________ __________ racism.	Wir müssen **Haltung gegenüber** Rassismus zeigen.
7 Who _____ _________ sportsperson of the year?	Wer **wurde zum/zur** Sportler/in des Jahres **ernannt**?
8 He was _____________ _____ his reaction.	Er wurde **wegen** seiner Reaktion **kritisiert**.
9 Toni and Felix play on ____________ teams.	Toni und Felix spielen in **gegnerischen** Mannschaften.
10 We saw lots of funny ______ in the zoo.	Wir sahen viele lustige **Menschenaffen** im Zoo.
11 You have the best view from the front _____.	Von der ersten **Reihe** sieht man am besten.
12 I was very ________ by his words.	Ich war wegen seiner Worte sehr **gekränkt**.

25 More about Sydney

Complete the text with words from the box.

Aboriginal • abroad • addition • attraction • business • capital • convicts • events • foreign • human • landmarks • natural • population • settled • tools • transformed • waterfront

The first people who lived in the area we know as Sydney probably came from northern Australia. **1** ____________ stone **2** ____________ have been discovered that show evidence of **3** ____________ activity in the area since about 50,000 years ago. Sydney is the **4** ____________ of New South Wales – but not of the country – and surrounds the world's largest **5** ____________ harbour, which is why the **6** ____________ is the main **7** ____________ of the city. The first Europeans who **8** ____________ there were the British. However, the city has **9** ____________ from a destination for **10** ____________ into a major international centre. It has a **11** ____________ of around 4.5 million, and 1.5 million of these were born **12** ____________: more than 250 different languages are spoken in Sydney. Sydney is also open for **13** ____________.

It is home to many **14** ____________ banks, and has hosted **15** ____________ such as the 2000 summer Olympics. In **16** ____________, millions of tourists visit the city each year to see the famous **17** ____________.

26 Words and phrases → (pp. 27–29)

1 How did the team celebrate their __________?	Wie hat die Mannschaft ihren **Sieg** gefeiert?
2 I didn't hear the player's __________.	Ich hörte die **Bemerkung** des Spielers nicht.
3 She didn't do it. She's __________.	Sie hat es nicht gemacht. Sie ist **unschuldig**.
4 You _____ the _________ ____ me ____ everything!	Du **gibst** mir **an** allem die **Schuld**!
5 __________ we can't come to your party.	Wir können **leider** nicht zu eurem Fest kommen.
6 Dad was __________ as a child. It was horrible.	Vati wurde als Kind **gemobbt**. Es war furchtbar.
7 Their __________ shows they're brothers.	Ihr **Aussehen** zeigt, dass sie Brüder sind.
8 My uncle works in the coal __________.	Mein Onkel arbeitet in der Kohle**industrie**.
9 I always enjoy her __________.	Ich genieße immer ihre **Gesellschaft**.
10 The police are investigating the __________.	Die Polizei untersucht gerade den **Vorfall**.
11 The fans __________ the other team.	Die Fans **buhten** die andere Mannschaft **aus**.
12 My first book was a big __________.	Mein erstes Buch war eine große **Errungenschaft**.
13 *Doctor Who* is a very old TV __________.	*Doctor Who* ist eine sehr alte Fernseh**serie**.
14 The book's __________ is London 100 years ago.	Der **Schauplatz** des Buches ist London vor 100 Jahren.

27 The right word

Circle the correct word to complete the sentences.

1 She's wearing the winner's **award** • **achievement** • **medal** she got in the Olympics.

2 It's normal, but I disagree with fans who boo the **opposed** • **opposing** • **opposite** team.

3 If you sit in the front **line** • **row** • **rank** you get a fantastic view of the game.

4 **I'm afraid of** • **Luckily** • **Unfortunately** bullying is still a problem in many schools.

5 It's important to **stand up for** • **debate** • **be determined for** what you believe is right.

6 Everyone should **take a stand against** • **put the blame on** • **criticize** racism.

7 We had a very **live** • **lively** • **living** lesson when we debated problems in society.

8 I'm not against soccer players' high salaries; others **take** • **make** • **find** a different view.

9 He made a **hurtful** • **talkative** • **descriptive** comment that really upset me.

10 People in rural areas say cities are **overcrowdy** • **overcrowding** • **overcrowded** .

28 Crossword

Across →
1 friend
3 area of a city
8 desert animal
10 badly hurt
12 far away
14 with too many people
15 used to stop burning
19 breathe in the sea
21 the way sb./sth. looks
22 words that go together to make a useful expression
23 to be against something

Down ↓
2 to change completely
4 animal with eight legs
5 a place to grow flowers and vegetables
6 fashionable
7 not public
8 say negative things about
9 a long snake
11 a meal cooked outdoors (AusE)
12 not polite
13 dangerous animal in rivers and the sea
16 football
17 animal that jumps a lot
18 where the sea meets the land
19 big white bird
20 very beautiful
24 someone a doctor helps

2 Unit

Relationships

1 Words and phrases ➜ (pp. 34–36)

1 Dad is a very good ________.	Vati ist ein sehr guter **Fotograf**.
2 I'm reading a ______ in English.	Ich lese gerade einen **Roman** auf Englisch.
3 I ________ I know all the people in my village.	Ich **schätze**, ich kenne alle Leute in meinem Dorf.
4 He must come. He made me a ________.	Er muss kommen. Er hat mir ein **Versprechen** gegeben.
5 After the swim, my lips were ______.	Nach dem Schwimmen waren meine Lippen **salzig**.
6 An Indian doctor ________ her after her accident.	Ein indischer Arzt **behandelte** sie nach ihrem Unfall.
7 Tomorrow I'm going to get a new ________.	Morgen bekomme ich einen neuen **Haarschnitt**.
8 OK, eat my chips. ________ ______ ____ ____.	OK, iss meine Pommes. **Von mir aus gern**.
9 Did you ______ in the last ________?	**Hast** du in den letzten **Wahlen gewählt**?
10 His favourite ________ is ________.	Sein Lieblings**thema** ist die **Politik**.
11 He is very ________ about his thin hair.	Er ist wegen seinen dünnen Haaren sehr **empfindlich**.
12 What is the biggest ______ in in your family?	Was ist die größte **Streitfrage** in deiner Familie?
13 ______ we were in the car, I remembered my phone.	**Sobald** wir im Auto waren, dachte ich an mein Handy.
14 Are all computer games a ______ of time?	Sind alle Computerspiele eine Zeit**verschwendung**?

2 The right words

Choose the correct words from the box to complete these sentences.

elections · fine · haircut · novel · once · politics · promise · reckon · sensitive · subject · treat · vote · waste

1 I ________ you can have my ________ ________ I have finished it.

2 Don't talk about ________. It's such a boring ________.

3 It's time for a me to get a ________, I ________.

4 If you don't to ________, that's ________ by me.

5 I watched a terrible programme about the recent ________. It was a ________ of time.

6 People can be ________, so you should ________ everyone with kindness.

3 Words and phrases ➜ *(p. 37)*

1 I didn't see the ______ ______ in the dark.	Im Dunkeln sah ich den **Baumstamm** nicht.
2 I fell, hurt my ______ and ______ my jeans.	Ich fiel, verletzte mein **Kinn** und **zerriß** meine Jeans.
3 The ______ on my phone are too small.	Die **Tasten** meines Handys sind zu klein.
4 I was so nervous that my hands ______.	Ich war so nervös, dass meine Hände **zitterten**.
5 Everyone should learn ______ ______ in school.	Alle sollten in der Schule **Erste Hilfe** lernen.
6 Nobody can ______ under water.	Niemand kann unter Wasser **atmen**.
7 The ______ on his hands was very hard.	Die **Haut** an seinen Händen war sehr hart.
8 After the race her ______ were very red.	Nach dem Rennen waren ihre **Wangen** sehr rot.
9 How fast is the average ______?	Wie schnell ist der durchscnittliche **Puls**?
10 The ______ needs ______ to work.	Das **Gehirn** braucht **Sauerstoff**, um zu funktionieren.
11 Their village is very ______ from other towns.	Ihr Dorf ist weit **entfernt** von anderen Städten.
12 The boat started to ______ in the storm.	Das Boot begann im Sturm zu **sinken**.
13 Who is the most ______ boy in your class?	Wer ist der **intelligenteste** Junge in deiner Klasse?
14 We ______ go out for a nice meal.	Wir gehen **ab und zu** schön essen.

4 Logic!

Match the two parts logically.

1 The message contained some spelling mistakes.
2 I wouldn't say she's a friend of mine.
3 I don't think there is much sugar in this.
4 I don't like swimming very much.
5 The photo is not very clear at all.
6 I'm sure I'm not dead.
7 I just can't think of the answer.
8 I wanted to say something intelligent.
9 I don't think he's a farmer, you know.
10 You shouldn't stare at people.

a To be honest, I sink.
b My hands were shaking at the time.
c It's rude. How would you like it?
d However, I couldn't think of anything.
e I think his skin is too soft for that.
f We just meet occasionally.
g My brain's not working today.
h I hit the wrong key a few times.
i In fact it tastes very salty.
j But I can't find my pulse.

5 Words and phrases ➜ *(pp. 37–38)*

1 She always has a __________ expression.	Sie hat immer einen **verträumten** Ausdruck.
2 We saw pictures of __________ on TV.	Wir sahen Bilder von **Einwanderern** im Fernsehen.
3 I don't know if I want to go to __________.	Ich weiß nicht, ob ich auf die **Universität** gehen will.
4 I want to buy some ______ and __________.	Ich will **Seife** und **Deodorant** kaufen.
5 I need a new __________ too.	Ich brauche auch eine neue **Zahnbürste**.
6 Where's the __________?	Wo ist die **Zahnpasta**?
7 The ________ isn't the place for ______.	Der **Kühlschrank** ist nicht der Ort für **Dosen**.
8 It was ________ cold, but we swam ________.	Es war **ziemlich** kalt, aber wir schwammen **trotzdem**.
9 I'm not very __________ with this area.	Ich bin mit dieser Gegend nicht sehr **vertraut**.
10 There was an __________ silence.	Es gab eine **unangenehme** Stille.
11 What's happening ______ ______?	Was passiert **nebenan**?

6 Missing!

Complete the words with the missing letters.

1 I like the smell of your _ _ _ **d o** _ _ _ _ _.

2 Do you have to pay to go to _ _ _ **v e** _ _ _ _ _ _ in Australia?

3 I felt very _ _ **k w** _ _ _ when they started arguing in front of me.

4 Don't talk about exams. It's a _ _ _ _ **i t** _ _ _ subject with him.

5 Can I borrow some _ _ _ _ **h p** _ _ _ _? I forgot mine.

6 Most nights I stay in, but _ _ _ _ **s i** _ _ _ _ _ _ I go to the cinema with friends.

7 Some people think there are too many _ _ _ _ **g r** _ _ _ _ in the country.

8 It was difficult to _ _ _ **a t** _ _ because of the smoke.

9 It's always nice to see a _ _ _ _ **l i** _ _ face when you are in a new place.

10 Is it true that plants produce _ _ _ **g e** _?

7 Words and phrases ➜ *(pp. 39–42)*

1 You want ___________? Do more sport.	Du willst **Muskeln** haben? Treibe mehr Sport!
2 I couldn't see the ________ of my watch.	Ich konnte die **Zeiger** meiner Uhr nicht sehen.
3 I _________ to tell you later.	Ich **hatte die Absicht**, es dir später zu sagen.
4 I'm nervous ___________ ____ the test.	Ich bin **wegen** der Klassenarbeit nervös.
5 This is a __________ problem.	Das ist ein **ernstes** Problem.
6 I like _______-________ ____________.	Ich mag **Ich-Erzählungen**.
7 Can I make a ___________?	Kann ich eine **Bitte** äußern?
8 The way they spoke was very ____________.	Wie sie redeten, war sehr **umgangssprachlich**.
9 Moths are _____________ ____ lamps.	Nachtfalter **fühlen sich** zu Lampen **hingezogen**.
10 He _____ ___ ______ as soon as he ________ her.	Er **verliebte sich**, sobald er **mit** ihr **ging**.
11 Did you know Max ___ _______ Kate again?	Wusstest du, dass Max wieder **mit** Kate **zusammen ist**?
12 I thought they had __________ ____.	Ich dachte, sie hätten **sich getrennt**.
13 I _____ ___ ______ Jon playing football.	Ich **lernte** Jon beim Fußballspielen **kennen**.
14 I'm a bit ___________ ______ you, to be honest.	Um ehrlich zu sein: Ich bin etwas **verärgert über** dich.

8 That's wrong!

Circle the mistake(s) in each line and write the correct word(s) on the right. One line is correct – which?

1 He made a promiss not to talk about it as it's a sensative issue. ____________________

2 I don't spend any time argueing about politics. It's a waist of time. ____________________

3 He was very annoyed when I used his toothepaste. ____________________

4 Sorry, I ment to phone you but I just forget. ____________________

5 My brother is learning about first-person naratives at uniwersity. ____________________

6 Ocasionally he can say something inteligent, you know. ____________________

7 The mussels in your body need oxigene to work properly. ____________________

8 They made a serious request to have an informal meeting. ____________________

9 He was starring at the wall with a dreemy expression on his face. ____________________

10 My hands were shacking when I started my first haarcut. ____________________

9 Words and phrases ➔ (p. 42)

1 Because he looked __________, I explained again.	Weil er **verwirrt** aussah, erklärte ich es noch einmal.
2 I'm not annoyed – I'm really ________ _______ her.	Ich bin nicht verärgert – ich bin richtig **sauer auf** sie.
3 It's safe. You don't need to be __________.	Es ist sicher. Du musst nicht **verängstigt** sein.
4 The dog looked at us with __________ eyes.	Der Hund sah uns mit **hoffnungsvollen** Augen an.
5 __________ the rain will stop soon.	**Hoffentlich** hört der Regen bald auf.
6 Don't be so __________ about everything!	Sei nicht so **pessimistisch** wegen allem!
7 I'm really __________ with the results.	Ich bin über die Ergebnisse wirklich **erfreut**.
8 If you tell him, he'll be ________ _______ you.	Wenn du es ihm sagst, wird er **wütend auf** dich sein.
9 He was __________ when Jane left him.	Er war **todunglücklich**, als Jane ihn verließ.
10 Aunt Elvira ___ __________ ___ spiders.	Tante Elvira **hat schreckliche Angst vor** Spinnen.

10 Three into one

Join the three parts (one from each column) to make sentences.

1 They met a few times, then	a seeing each other	I in love almost immediately.
2 I thought he might be cross, but he	b attracted	II Jim until we played football together
3 I'm really pleased they are	c terrified	III to her, to be honest.
4 He was really confused by what	d voted	IV for making that silly mistake.
5 I used to be really	e annoyed with myself	V dating but have now broken up.
6 I didn't mean to	f happened	VI as I'm actually quite hopeful.
7 I didn't really get to	g wasn't,	VII because they are a lovely couple.
8 They met and	h sound pessimistic,	VIII of flying, but I'm much better now.
9 I found it difficult to	i know	IX he was absolutely furious.
10 He asked me how I	j started	X in the last elections.
11 I like her, but I'm not	k fell	XI because he didn't understand.
12 When I realized, I was very	l breathe	XII because of the thick smoke.

11 Words and phrases ➜ *(pp. 42–43)*

1 She was ________ when he invited her to dinner.	Sie war **begeistert**, als er sie zum Essen einlud.
2 The house was ________ empty.	Das Haus war **absolut** leer.
3 He doesn't talk to his ____-wife any more.	Er redet nicht mehr mit seiner **Ex**-Frau.
4 These plants are both ________ and ________.	Diese Pflanzen sind sowohl **männlich** als auch **weiblich**.
5 He's only an ________, not a friend.	Er ist nur ein **Bekannter**, kein Freund.
6 Please ________ your address on the form.	**Tragen** Sie bitte Ihre Adresse in das Formular **ein**.
7 Help, I've forgotten my ________.	Hilfe, ich habe mein **Passwort** vergessen.
8 I ________ my ________ yesterday.	Ich **aktualisierte** meinen **Status** gestern.
9 He has an ________ with a bank in Switzerland.	Er hat ein **Konto** bei einer Bank in der Schweiz.

12 Almost the same

Match the sentences with similar meanings.

1 She had a bad time when they broke up.
2 She's been seeing him for a while.
3 She used to be his girlfriend.
4 That's the bank she uses.
5 I know her a little, but we're not friends.
6 The news was brilliant.
7 She always expects things to go wrong.
8 She doesn't understand what you mean.
9 She really wasn't very happy.
10 She was really angry.
11 She'll be really pleased with that.
12 She entered all her details.

a She was thrilled.
b She's his ex.
c She was absolutely furious.
d She has an account with them.
e She's a bit confused.
f She was quite cross.
g She completed the form.
h She's an acquaintance.
i She's dating him.
j She was heartbroken.
k She's such a pessimist.
l She'll like that, I'm sure.

13 Words and phrases ➔ (pp. 44–46)

1 There was a __________ in London yesterday.	Gestern gab es in London einen **Mord**.
2 When did the US __________ independence?	Wann **erklärten** die USA die Unabhängigkeit?
3 Jim and Gemma are __________ and ______.	Jim und Gemma sind **Ehemann** und **Ehefrau**.
4 The doctor said Dad ________ ____ stop smoking.	Der Arzt sagte, Vati **sollte** mit dem Rauchen aufhören.
5 Fruit is important for my ______.	Obst ist wichtig für meine **Ernährungsweise**.
6 I can't eat that - I'm on a ______.	Ich kann das nicht essen: Ich mache gerade **Diät**.
7 There's a lot of __________ in meat.	Im Fleisch ist viel **Eiweiß**.
8 You need to eat well to stay __________.	Man muss gut essen, um **gesund** zu bleiben.
9 The work is ____________ ____ finish tomorrow.	Die Arbeit **soll** morgen fertig werden.
10 They eat a lot of ________ in Italy.	Man isst in Italien viele **Nudeln**.
11 Let's do something __________ tonight.	Machen wir etwas **Kulturelles** heute Abend.
12 They had ____________________ problems in Spain.	Sie hatten **Kommunikations**probleme in Spanien.

14 Quiz time!

1 Where do you keep food fresh in the kitchen?

____

2 What's the fourth word: brother: sister; wife:…

____

3 You can clean yourself with this.

____

4 You keep your money in this in a bank.

____

5 The opposite of male.

____

6 A food, like pizza, that is popular in Italy.

____

7 The opposite of formal.

____

8 A type of book that people read for pleasure.

____

9 The main part of a tree that supports the branches.

____

10 The act of killing a person illegally.

____

11 The part of your face below your mouth.

____

12 You need this to protect your online accounts.

____

15 Words and phrases ➔ *(p. 47)*

1 There are different sorts of ______.	Es gibt verschiedene Arten von **Statistik**.
2 ____ ______ compare different numbers.	**Balkendiagramme** vergleichen verschiedene Zahlen.
3 ____ ______ show parts of a whole thing.	**Tortendiagramme** zeigen Teile eines Ganzen.
4 I don't understand this ______.	Ich verstehe dieses **Schaubild** nicht.
5 The ______ person sleeps 8 hours a night.	Der **Durchschnitts**mensch schläft 8 Stunden pro Nacht.
6 The official ______ of a marathon is 26.2 miles.	Die offizielle **Länge** des Marathons ist 42,195 km.
7 Is it ______ to know when you will die?	Ist es **nützlich** zu wissen, wann man stirbt?
8 What ______ of Germans have no jobs?	Welcher **Prozentsatz** der Deutschen hat keine Arbeit?
9 Should you do ______ to earn money?	Sollte man **Hausarbeit** leisten, um Geld zu verdienen?
10 I suddenly ______ that she was unhappy.	Ich **erkannte** plötzlich, dass sie unglücklich war.
11 Grandma always ______ ____ us eating enough.	Oma **besteht** immer **darauf**, dass wir genug essen.

16 One from two

Match the two parts to complete the sentences.

1 I can't go out at the weekend until I've finished
2 What worries me about the bike ride is
3 Healthy eating is very important for
4 When I meet friends, I shake hands or kiss on
5 I was thirsty so I went to the fridge and took out
6 I'm not sure about buying that watch. I don't like
7 He's never asked for anything, so I was surprised by
8 All the information you need is in
9 What worries me about living abroad is
10 The scariest scene in the film is
11 Nobody can get into my account without
12 You need public transport to get to

a the cheek.
b the request.
c the password.
d the murder.
e the pie chart.
f the chores.
g the skin.
h the hands.
i the length.
j the university.
k the can.
l the communication.

17 Words and phrases ➜ (pp. 48–49)

1 We have a small ________ of salt – is it enough?	Wir haben eine kleine **Menge** Salz – reicht das?
2 Different cultures have different ________.	Verschiedene Kulturen haben verschiedene **Werte**.
3 How ______ is your room?	Wie **ordentlich** ist dein Zimmer?
4 I don't have any ______ – can you lend me some?	Ich habe kein **Bargeld** – kannst du mir etwas leihen?
5 It's ________ not true that young people are lazy.	Es ist **einfach** nicht wahr, dass junge Leute faul sind.
6 Quick! We're ________ ______ ____ time.	Schnell! Wir **haben keine** Zeit **mehr**.
7 ____________ him – __________ he'll learn.	**Ermutige** ihn – **vielleicht** lernt er.
8 _________ ________ are good; others are bad.	**Gewisse Gewohnheiten** sind gut, andere schlecht.
9 When was the trade ____________ signed?	Wann wurde die Handels**vereinbarung** unterschrieben?
10 He gave me a chance to ________ myself fully.	Er gab mir die Gelegenheit, mich voll **auszudrücken**.
11 I must _______ that it is your decision.	Ich muss **betonen**: Es ist Ihre Entscheidung.
12 We have ______ at home. We love eggs!	Wir haben **Hennen** zu Hause. Wir lieben Eier!
13 We ________ ____ _______.	Wir **sahen ein, dass wir uns nicht einigen konnten**.
14 Please ________ me to go to the bank.	**Erinnere** mich bitte, dass ich zur Bank muss.

18 Missing!

Add missing words to **two** of the **four** gaps to complete the sentences.

1 We weren't going to reach ________ agreement ________ , so we ________ had to agree ________ disagree.

2 Many ________ families insist ________ ________ kids doing ________ chores if they want pocket money.

3 If you ________ want to get ________ job and not go to ________ university, that's fine ________ me.

4 The car hit ________ tree ________ trunk, but fortunately there ________ no ________ serious damage.

5 I've been staring ________ this crossword puzzle ________ hours ________ but I just ________ can't do it.

6 I'm really ________ pleased ________ the mark I got for ________ narrative I wrote for ________ school.

7 We're a little ________ late ________ because ________ the traffic, but ________ least we have arrived.

8 I'm generally attracted ________ ________ people who have ________ positive take on ________ things.

19 Words and phrases ➜ (p. 50)

1 I can't imagine life as a ____________.	Ich kann mir das Leben als **Flüchtling** nicht vorstellen.
2 William plays in the ________ team.	William spielt in der **Jugend**mannschaft.
3 I work for a government ________________.	Ich arbeite bei einer Regierungs**organisation**.
4 I want to _____ my own business later.	Später will ich mein eigenes Geschäft **leiten**.
5 She ____________ her first novel at 17.	Sie **veröffentlichte** ihren ersten Roman mit 17.
6 Your ______________ is very important to me.	Deine **Freundschaft** ist mir sehr wichtig.
7 We had to _____ _____ a _______ when we arrived.	Wir mussten ein **Formular ausfüllen**, als wir ankamen.
8 The ____________ to the city is 10 miles.	Die **Entfernung** zur Stadt ist 16 km.

20 Scrambled report

Put the parts in the correct order. The first one has been done for you.

a There are a lot of stories about immigrants and

c left behind everything they are familiar with and that they

e in or maybe even will not want to try to adapt to

d people who come from cultures which have very different

j to work and make a contribution; and we must remember that

f on TV these days: it's one of the most sensitive

g and the habits of their own country. Others disagree and

b ought to be treated with respect and given our

i values as perhaps they will find it difficult to fit

l say it is our responsibility to help these people who have

n their new society but will keep their language, religion

k issues we have today. Some people say that we should not accept

m friendship. It's important to realize that immigrants want

o many refugees travel great distances to be safe and not feel terrified every day.

h refugees published in the newspapers and shown

Answer: a ☐ ☐ ☐ ☐ ☐ ☐ ☐ ☐ ☐ ☐ ☐ ☐ ☐ ☐

21 Words and phrases ➜ *(p. 50)*

1 He always travels by public ______________.	Er fährt immer mit öffentlichen **Verkehrsmitteln**.
2 The first problem he ________ was the language.	Das erste Problem, das **vor ihm stand**, war die Sprache.
3 It's hard to _____ ____ without English.	Ohne Englisch ist es schwer, **sich einzufügen**.
4 You're not a child. _____ like a man.	Du bist kein Kind mehr. **Verhalte dich** wie ein Mann.
5 You'll soon _________ to the culture.	Du wirst **dich** schnell der Kultur **anpassen**.
6 I soon _____ _______ ____ speaking English.	Ich **gewöhnte mich** schnell **daran**, Englisch zu sprechen.
7 I missed the bus and _________ ____ ___________.	Ich verpasste den Bus und **bin schließlich gelaufen**.

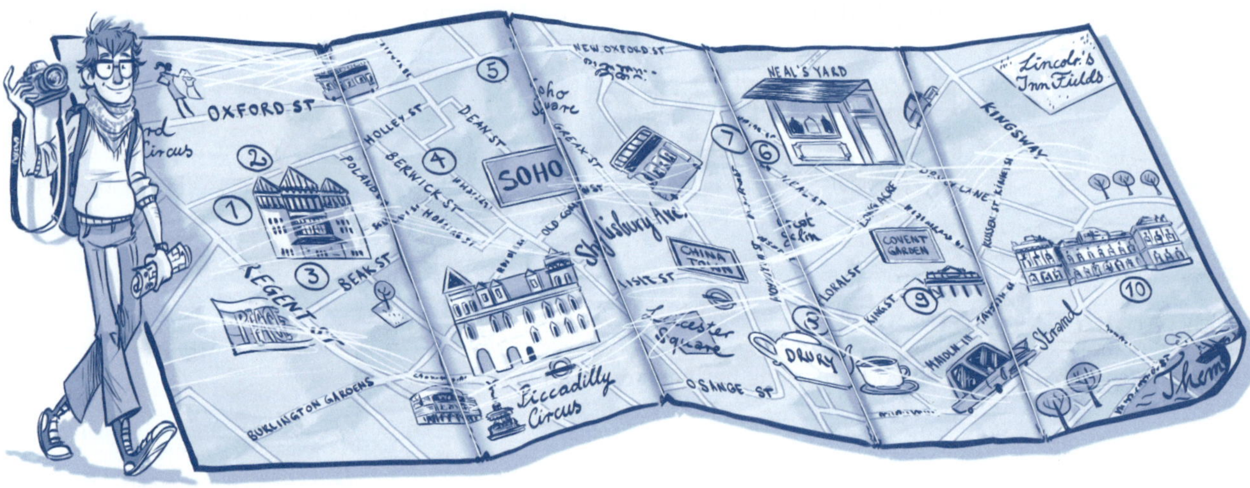

22 Keywords

Rewrite the sentences using the keywords so they mean the same as the original.
Don't change the keyword in any way.

1 We haven't got any more eggs.	out	______________
2 I didn't forget it was her birthday because he told me.	reminded	______________
3 I don't eat everything because I don't want to be so fat.	on	______________
4 The moon is about 400,000 km from the Earth.	between	______________
5 We went for a swim in the sea although it was cold.	anyway	______________
6 My parents were unhappy that my hair was too long.	length	______________
7 I hated the hotel at first, but now it's not a problem.	got	______________
8 After a while, we had an argument.	ended	______________
9 There will be a big problem for us soon.	facing	______________
10 I don't have much money.	amount	______________

23 Words and phrases ➜ (p. 50)

1 Take ________________ for your actions.	Übernimm die **Verantwortung** für deine Handlungen.
2 He managed to find a job ________ 13 days.	Er schaffte es, **innerhalb von** 13 Tagen Arbeit zu finden.
3 I asked an _________ for help.	Ich bat einen **Berater** um Hilfe.
4 He works as a _______ for old people.	Er arbeitet als **Pfleger** für alte Leute.
5 A baby is totally _____________ ____ its mother.	Ein Baby ist total **abhängig von** seiner Mutter.
6 We _____ ____ _____ Beyoncé in 2016.	Wir **hatten** 2016 **die Möglichkeit**, Beyoncé **zu sehen**.
7 We ________ go ___________ last year.	Wir **sind** letztes Jahr **nirgendwohin** gereist.

24 A conversation

Put the replies in this dialogue in the correct order.

1 What's the matter? You look upset. Are you cross about something?

2 Really? Why? You normally do well above average in all your subjects.

3 You mean the bar charts and the pie charts?

4 Well, don't worry. Perhaps you did better than you think.

5 Don't be so pessimistic. Perhaps your teacher will be pleased with your work.

6 But it's his job to encourage you. And he knows you're intelligent

7 Don't say that.

a I know, but this time I had problems with the statistics we had to do.

b Am I? It made me realize that I don't think I can go to university.

c I'm not sure about that. I didn't do everything we were supposed to do.

d I'm pretty sure he won't. He insists on nice tidy work with a good amount of detail.

e Well, I'm just annoyed with myself because of the homework. I only got a "D".

f Yes. I took too long doing my chores and then simply ran out of time.

25 Words and phrases ➜ (p. 51)

1 I saw it in the ______ ________.	Ich sah es im **Schaufenster**.
2 I never wear an ________ when I cook.	Ich trage nie eine **Schürze**, wenn ich koche.
3 Why _____ you ___ such ___ _______?	Warum **hast** du **es** so **eilig**?
4 We ____________ eat around 7 pm.	Wir essen **normalerweise** gegen 19:00 Uhr.
5 My legs are _______ after that walk yesterday.	Meine Beine sind nach dem gestrigen Spaziergang **steif**.
6 We all played football, ____________ my grandma.	Wir spielten alle Fußball, **einschließlich** meiner Oma.
7 We did the work in __________.	Wir haben die Arbeit im **Tandem** gemacht.
8 Heathrow is an important _____ for aeroplanes.	Heathrow ist ein wichtiger **Knotenpunkt** für Flugzeuge.
9 Everything here is _____________.	Alles hier ist **handgemacht**.

26 The right word

(Circle) the correct word to complete the sentences.

1 I'll be very **cross** • **crossed** • **crossing** with you if you are late again.

2 He's not **normalwise** • **normally** • **normal** so sensitive about things like that.

3 This tastes very **saltish** • **salted** • **salty** . Let's add some more water.

4 He was quiet, but he was nice when you got to **knowing** • **known** • **know** him.

5 My dad has two **hairscuts** • **haircuts** • **haircuttings** a month. He likes short hair.

6 I haven't changed my profile for ages. I ought to **update** • **redate** • **actual** it.

7 My friends paid for my whole holiday, **include** • **included** • **including** the flights.

8 In cities, it's common not to know the people who live **near** • **next** • **beside** door.

9 I don't think politics **is** • **are** boring. I find **them** • **it** really interesting.

10 To join the club, all you have to do is **complete** • **fill** • **write** in a form.

11 Slow down! Why are you in such **an** • **a** • **the** hurry? We've got plenty of time.

12 I think you should have more **diet** • **muscle** • **protein** in your food.

Lösungen

Unit 1

1 Words and phrases

1 region 2 bush 3 coral 4 kangaroo 5 outback 6 spiders 7 coastal 8 exotic 9 humid 10 remote 11 stunning 12 tropical 13 tropics 14 urban

2 The right words

1 tropical; stunning 2 humid; tropics 3 kangaroos; exotic 4 remote; outback 5 spiders; urban

3 Words and phrases

1 Aboriginal 2 camel 3 convicts 4 Koalas 5 poisonous 6 exchange 7 flight 8 lively 9 historical 10 quarter 11 settled 12 trendy 13 business district

4 Match the parts

1 c 2 a 3 e 4 j 5 g 6 d 7 i 8 b 9 f 10 h

5 Words and phrases

1 flying fox 2 foxes 3 opera 4 quay 5 half-hour 6 two-week 7 waterfront 8 guided 9 honest 10 take 11 Catch

6 Wrong!

1 ten-hour/remotest 2 trendy/quarter 3 convicts 4 coastal/coral 5 kangaroos/camels 6 exotic/poisonous 7 correct 8 Opera 9 business/attractions 10 correct 11 honest/urban 12 Aboriginal

7 Words and phrases

1 scenic 2 transformed 3 landmark 4 paradise 5 bay 6 Back then 7 Aussie 8 were 9 though 10 barbecue/barbie 11 board 12 swallow 13 tons 14 private

8 Fitting everything together

1 ~~stunning~~ private 2 ~~catch~~ transform 3 ~~paradise~~ landmark 4 ~~private~~ stunning 5 ~~surfer's board~~ paradise 6 ~~landmark~~ board 7 ~~tons~~ barbecues 8 ~~barbecues~~ tons 9 ~~swallow~~ catch 10 ~~transform~~ swallow

9 Words and phrases

1 accepted 2 talkative 3 photography 4 in the end 5 was; homesick 6 Christmas Eve 7 self-confident 8 easy-going 9 very first 10 sunscreen

10 Three into one

1 e+VI 2 g+IV 3 a+I 4 b+VII 5 f+II 6 h+III 7 c+VIII 8 d+V

11 Quick quiz

1 barbie 2 Aussie 3 Christmas Eve 4 sunscreen 5 photography

12 Words and phrases

1 No worries 2 mates 3 Argumentative; arguments 4 argumentative writing 5 argued 6 brainstorm 7 oppose 8 stating 9 abroad 10 In addition to 11 Personally 12 discuss

13 Almost the same

1 h 2 e 3 j 4 a 5 b 6 g 7 c 8 d 9 f 10 i

14 Words and phrases

1 Furthermore 2 in my view 3 On the one hand
4 On the other hand 5 take a different view
6 advantage 7 disadvantage 8 make comparisons
9 To start/begin with 10 Firstly 11 Secondly
12 Thirdly

15 Fill the gaps

1 addition to 2 in view 3 other hand 4 take view
5 the tropics 6 settled in 7 Back then 8 To with

16 Words and phrases

1 reef 2 flooded 3 determined to 4 insects
5 python 6 Luckily 7 prefer; to; humans 8 mainly
9 provoke 10 injured; moths 11 crocodiles
12 bump into 13 snorkelled

17 Talking about presentations

1 e 2 h 3 a 4 g 5 c 6 j 7 d 8 i 9 f 10 b

18 Words and phrases

1 greenhouse 2 coastline 3 dramatic 4 facilities are
5 overcrowded 6 Rural 7 Suburban 8 vast
9 inland 10 mild 11 mountainous 12 old-fashioned 13 flat 14 descriptive 15 Collocations

19 Keywords

1 a 24-hour supermarket. 2 your take on the plan?
3 great idea in my view. 4 my very first time abroad.
5 determined to win. 6 take a different view.

20 Words and phrases

1 disagree 2 rude; hurtful 3 nonsense 4 share
5 totally 6 I'm afraid 7 have a point 8 gift token
9 So can 10 So does 12 So would

21 Scrambled report

1 a 2 e 3 g 4 c 5 j 6 f 7 i 8 d 9 l 10 k
11 b 12 h 13 m

22 Words and phrases

1 sort of 2 soccer 3 is digging 4 opportunity
5 possibility 6 work experience 7 clinic 8 patients
9 debated 10 racism 11 racist 12 professional

23 Missing!

1 –/–/of/to 2 the/of/–/– 3 –/who/that so/–
4 –/with/–/a 5 –/–/with/are 6 –/an/the/–
7 –/as/–/in 8 –/to/–/would

24 Words and phrases

1 swans 2 medal 3 award 4 stood up for
5 recognition 6 stand against 7 was named
8 criticized for 9 opposing 10 apes 11 row
12 upset

25 More about Sydney

1 Aboriginal 2 tools 3 human 4 capital 5 natural
6 waterfront 7 attraction 8 settled 9 transformed
10 convicts 11 population 12 abroad 13 business
14 foreign 15 events 16 addition 17 landmarks

26 Words and phrases

1 victory 2 comment 3 innocent 4 put blame on; for 5 Unfortunately 6 bullied 7 appearance
8 industry 9 society 10 incident 11 booed
12 achievement 13 series 14 setting

27 The right word

1 medal 2 opposing 3 row 4 Unfortunately
5 stand up for 6 stand against 7 lively 8 take
9 hurtful 10 overcrowded

28 Crossword

Across
1 mate 3 quarter 8 camel 10 injured 12 remote
14 overcrowded 15 sunscreen 19 snorkel
21 appearance 22 collocation 23 oppose

Down
2 transform 4 spider 5 greenhouse 6 trendy
7 private 8 criticize 9 python 11 barbie 12 rude
13 crocodile 16 soccer 17 kangaroo 18 coastline
19 swan 20 stunning 24 patient

Unit 2

1 Words and phrases

1 photographer 2 novel 3 reckon 4 promise 5 salty 6 treated 7 haircut 8 Thats fine by me 9 vote; elections 10 subject; politics 11 sensitive 12 issue 13 Once 14 waste

2 The right words

1 promise; novel; once 2 politics; subject 3 haircut; reckon 4 vote; fine 5 elections; waste 6 sensitive; treat

3 Words and phrases

1 tree trunk 2 chin; tore 3 keys 4 shook 5 first aid 6 breathe 7 skin 8 cheeks 9 pulse 10 brain; oxygen 11 distant 12 sink 13 intelligent 14 occasionally

4 Logic!

1 h 2 f 3 i 4 a 5 b 6 j 7 g 8 d 9 e 10 c

5 Words and phrases

1 dreamy 2 immigrants 3 university 4 soap; deodorant 5 toothbrush 6 toothpaste 7 fridge; cans 8 pretty anyway 9 familiar 10 awkward 11 next door

6 Missing!

1 deodorant 2 university 3 awkward 4 sensitive 5 toothpaste 6 occasionally 7 immigrants 8 breathe 9 familiar 10 oxygen

7 Words and phrases

1 muscles 2 hands 3 meant 4 because of 5 serious 6 first-person narratives 7 request 8 informal 9 attracted to 10 fell in love; dated 11 is seeing 12 broken up 13 got to know 14 annoyed with

8 That's wrong!

1 promise; sensitive 2 arguing; waste 3 toothpaste 4 meant; forgot 5 narratives; university 6 Occasionally; intelligent 7 muscles; oxygen 8 correct 9 staring; dreamy 10 shaking; haircut

9 Words and phrases

1 confused 2 cross with 3 frightened 4 hopeful 5 Hopefully 6 pessimistic 7 pleased 8 furious with 9 heartbroken 10 is terrified of

10 Three into one

1 j+V 2 g+IX 3 a+VII 4 f+XI 5 c+VIII 6 h+VI 7 i+II 8 k+I 9 l+XII 10 d+X 11 b+III 12 e+IV

11 Words and phrases

1 thrilled 2 absolutely 3 ex- 4 male; female 5 acquaintance 6 enter 7 password 8 updated; status 9 account

12 Almost the same

1 j 2 i 3 b 4 d 5 h 6 a 7 k 8 e 9 f 10 c 11 l 12 g

13 Words and phrases

1 murder 2 declare 3 husband; wife 4 ought to 5 diet 6 diet 7 protein 8 healthy 9 supposed to 10 pasta 11 cultural 12 communication

14 Quiz time!

1 fridge **2** husband **3** soap **4** account **5** female **6** pasta **7** informal **8** novel **9** tree trunk **10** murder **11** chin **12** password

15 Words and phrases

1 statistics **2** Bar charts **3** Pie charts **4** chart **5** average **6** length **7** useful **8** percentage **9** chores **10** realized **11** insists on

16 One from two

1 f **2** i **3** g **4** a **5** k **6** h **7** b **8** e **9** l **10** d **11** c **12** j

17 Words and phrases

1 amount **2** values **3** tidy **4** cash **5** simply **6** running out of **7** Encourage; perhaps **8** Certain habits **9** agreement **10** express **11** stress **12** hens **13** agreed to differ **14** remind

18 Missing!

1 an/–/–/to **2** –/on/the, their/– **3** –/a/–/by **4** a, the/–/was, is/– **5** at/for/–/– **6** –/with/the/– **7** –/–/of/at **8** to/–/a/–

19 Words and phrases

1 refugee **2** youth **3** organization **4** run **5** published **6** friendship **7** fill in; form **8** distance

20 Scrambled report

1 a **2** h **3** f **4** k **5** d **6** i **7** e **8** n **9** g **10** l **11** c **12** b **13** m **14** j **15** o

21 Words and phrases

1 transport **2** he faced **3** fit in **4** Act **5** adapt **6** got used to **7** ended up walking

22 Keywords

Mögliche Lösungen:

1 We've run out of eggs. **2** He reminded me it was her birthday. **3** I'm on a diet. **4** The distance between the Moon and the Earth is about 400,000 km. **5** It was cold, but we went for a swim in the sea anyway. **6** My parents didn't like the length of my hair. **7** At first I didn't like the hotel, but now I've got used to it. **8** We ended up having an argument. **9** We are facing a big problem. **10** I only have a small amount of money.

23 Words and phrases

1 responsibility **2** within **3** advisor **4** carer **5** dependent on **6** got to see **7** didn't; anywhere

24 A conversation

1 e **2** a **3** f **4** c **5** d **6** b

25 Words and phrases

1 shop window **2** apron **3** are; in; a hurry **4** normally **5** stiff **6** including **7** tandem **8** hub **9** handmade

26 The right word

1 cross **2** normally **3** salty **4** know **5** haircuts **6** update **7** including **8** next **9** is/it **10** fill **11** a **12** protein

27 Dialogues

1 f **2** j **3** g **4** l **5** b **6** k **7** d **8** a **9** e **10** h **11** c **12** i

28 Missing!

1 first **2** dependent **3** heartbroken **4** windows **5** Hopefully **6** transport **7** advisor; encourage **8** agreement **9** remind; organization **10** normally; friendships

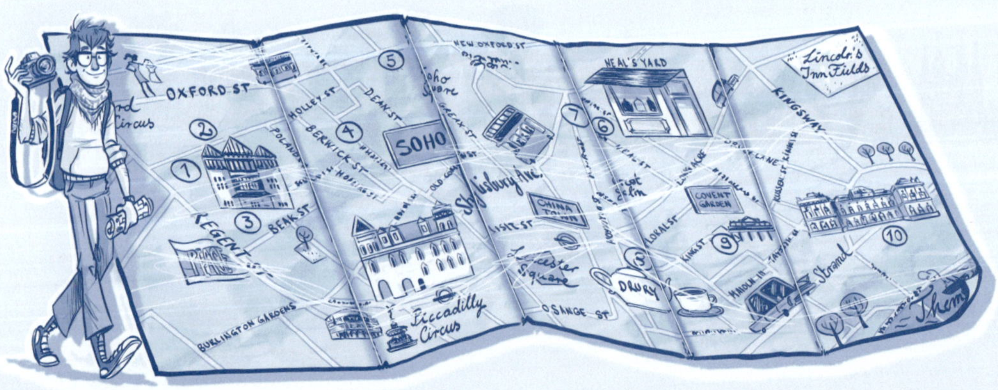

Unit 3

1 Words and phrases

1 army 2 athlete 3 global warming 4 make a difference 5 repair 6 scientific 7 skydiving 8 achieved 9 goals 10 deadline 11 failed 12 application 13 applied for

2 The right words

1 scientific; global warming 2 applying; army 3 goal; skydiving 4 difference; athletes 5 achieved; application 6 fail; repaired 7 deadline; applications

3 Words and phrases

1 excerpt 2 vice 3 former 4 about to 5 court 6 identical 7 shaved 8 pass 9 Bible; religious 10 bald 11 tell 12 embarrassing

4 Match the parts

1 e 2 d 3 i 4 b 5 c 6 j 7 f 8 a 9 g 10 h

5 Words and phrases

1 folded 2 match 3 flies; web 4 hand over 5 heat 6 sweat 7 neither; nor 8 cheat 9 ince 10 decent 11 matters 12 water pipes 13 burst

6 Q&A

1 k 2 f 3 g 4 b 5 j 6 a 7 l 8 d 9 c 10 h 11 e 12 i

7 Words and phrases

1 talent 2 intelligence 3 gift 4 Santa Claus 5 picked 6 stoplight 7 character 8 brave 9 competitive 10 crazy about 11 loyal 12 emotions 13 sense of humour 14 quality

8 That's wrong!

1 sense/humour 2 athletes/competitive 3 character/brave 4 talent/intelligence 5 embarrassing/ identical 6 decent 7 correct 8 neither/nor 9 court/repaired 10 correct

9 Words and phrases

1 particular 2 generous 3 hard-working; lazy 4 mean 5 tolerant of 6 suffixes 7 opposite 8 recognize 9 predictions 10 categories 11 canoeing; poetry

10 Three into one

1 f+IX 2 d+VI 3 t+X 4 g+I 5 h+V 6 k+VIII 7 j+II 8 b+IV 9 a+XI 10 e+XII 11 c+VII 12 l+III

11 Words and phrases

1 experiments 2 virus 3 diagnose 4 The more; the happier 5 refrigeration 6 lab 7 company 8 refused 9 chemicals 10 in time for

12 Almost the same

1 g 2 j 3 e 4 a 5 i 6 b 7 k 8 h 9 f 10 d 11 l 12 c

13 Words and phrases

1 passion 2 developed 3 current 4 submit; to 5 fair 6 includes 7 medicine 8 such as 9 motivation

14 Quiz time!

1 suffixes 2 bald 3 Santa Claus 4 skydiving 5 refuse 6 Vice president 7 fail 8 court 9 medicine 10 sweat 11 prediction 12 virus 13 emotion 14 lab/laboratory

15 Words and phrases

1 mouse 2 evolution 3 tackle 4 biology 5 equal 6 fur; thick 7 blind alley 8 having; painted 9 in the long term 10 understanding

16 One from two

1 g 2 e 3 a 4 c 5 i 6 b 7 j 8 d 9 f 10 h

17 Words and phrases

1 principle **2** do **3** succeed **4** announced
5 spontaneous **6** pirate **7** focuses **8** searched
9 save

18 Missing!

1 –/a/it **2** –/the/the **3** –/such/are **4** a/Neither/–
5 be/long/– **6** so/do/ – **7** my/–/have
8 to/–/included **9** –/in/for **10** a/–/of

19 Words and phrases

1 limit; to **2** carefully **3** produce **4** source
5 unless **6** quoted **7** quotation marks **8** gestures
9 mascot **10** marathon

20 Scrambled report

1 a **2** e **3** h **4** l **5** g **6** f **7** b **8** k **9** d
10 m **11** c **12** o **13** n **14** i **15** j

21 Words and phrases

1 sewn **2** creative **3** rely on **4** contact **5** damaged
6 trust **7** restores

22 Fill the gaps

1 rely; on **2** restored; again **3** marathon;too
4 focus; on **5** science; lab **6** tell; work **7** not; unless
8 do; since **9** principles; carefully **10** gesture; refused

23 Words and phrases

1 applicants **2** CV **3** personal **4** personal statement
5 statement **6** candidate **7** dates **8** reverse
9 terms **10** proofread **11** neighbourhood
12 increased

24 A conversation about CVs

1 g **2** e **3** b **4** a **5** f **6** c **7** d

25 Words and phrases

1 knowledge **2** to date **3** secondary school
4 primary school **5** qualification **6** felt craft
7 completion **8** IT **9** Roman

26 The right word

1 completion **2** applicants **3** Roman **4** knowledge
5 sewn **6** quotation **7** spontaneous **8** save
9 creative **10** on **11** emotion **12** proofreading
13 personal **14** thick

27 Keywords

Mögliche Lösungen:
1 Many people applied for the job. **2** At weekends, I limit the children to an hour a day on the computer. **3** He refuses to eat meat unless he knows where it's from. **4** The only way you can succeed in life is to work hard. **5** I like neither canoeing nor poetry. **6** There's an equal number of boys and girls in our class. **7** When my computer stopped working I had it repaired. **8** Illnesses such as the Ebola virus have killed many people. **9** Friday is the deadline for the project.

28 Missing!

1 knowledge; principles; refrigeration **2** personal; marathon **3** primary; secondary **4** neighbourhood; increased **5** statement; contribution; mascot
6 restoring; deadline

Unit 4

1 Words and phrases

1 It's up to 2 Antarctic 3 rose up 4 Collective 5 cycle 6 brought about 7 initiative 8 sign; petition 9 sit-in 10 march 11 go on strike 12 boycott; products

2 The right words

1 sign; petition 2 boycott; products 3 marches; sit-in 4 bring about; cycle 5 on strike; collective 6 initiative; Antarctic 7 up; you

3 Words and phrases

1 United Nations 2 conference 3 slowed down 4 installation; created 5 projected 6 All of a sudden 7 past 8 narrative; narrator 9 in progress 10 sight 11 by the time 12 are taking; break

4 Logic!

1 h 2 f 3 e 4 d 5 b 6 c 7 j 8 i 9 a 10 g

5 Words and phrases

1 interpret 2 contains 3 concerned about 4 depicts 5 comments on 6 analyse 7 Environmental; political 8 focuses on 9 cactus 10 effective 11 made 12 make 13 comes across

6 Missing!

1 environmental 2 political 3 interpret 4 narrative 5 effective 6 commenting 7 conference 8 boycott 9 concerned 10 contains

7 Words and phrases

1 take a stand on 2 threat 3 anonymous 4 Prime Minister 5 ministries 6 slaughter 7 anger 8 off the coast 9 cove 10 either; or 11 alcohol; licence 12 campaign 13 fine; owner 14 meeting; councillor

8 That's wrong!

1 anonymous/threat 2 coast/either 3 stand/slaughter 4 councillor/alcohol 5 owner/license 6 correct 7 campaign/across 8 anger/ministries 9 focus/interpret 10 hacked/worry

9 Words and phrases

1 deny 2 passed 3 risk 4 buy into 5 myth 6 gender 7 equality 8 reality; pay 9 safety 10 accident 11 survey

10 Three into one

1 d+VII 2 h+IV 3 g+I 4 a+X 5 b+VIII 6 j+III 7 i+IX 8 e+II 9 c+VI 10 f+V

11 Words and phrases

1 MP 2 take action 3 admit 4 is to 5 solution to 6 certainly 7 consider 8 considered buying 9 take up 10 helmet 11 am happy to

12 Almost the same

1 d 2 e 3 i 4 a 5 h 6 b 7 j 8 c 9 k 10 g 11 l 12 i

13 Words and phrases

1 weakened 2 weak 3 pain 4 raised 5 raised 6 raises 7 Do; feel like 8 feel like going 9 regretted 10 regret; starting 11 didn't; anywhere 12 not; anywhere 13 protested 14 after all

14 Quiz time!

1 helmet 2 deny 3 cactus 4 anger 5 regret 6 raise 7 anonymous 8 Prime Minister 9 protest 10 safety

15 Words and phrases

1 involvement **2** is getting; involved **3** senator; activist **4** activism **5** immigration **6** citizen **7** congress **8** democracy **9** demonstrated **10** discriminate against

16 One from two

1 g **2** h **3** i **4** a **5** b **6** k **7** l **8** c **9** j **10** e **11** d **12** f

17 Words and phrases

1 is based on **2** escape **3** violence **4** dawn **5** gathered **6** horrible **7** struggled **8** pyjamas **9** took; exam **10** line **11** appeal **12** demand; for **13** Home Office **14** department

18 The right word

1 in **2** on **3** about **4** after **5** else **6** action **7** on **8** up **9** on **10** to

19 Words and phrases

1 playground **2** riot **3** civil war **4** minority **5** persuaded **6** didn't take notice of **7** drew; attention **8** catch; attention **9** pay attention **10** cases **11** broadcast **12** use

20 More about activism

1 a **2** f **3** i **4** d **5** b **6** e **7** h **8** k **9** j **10** c **11** g

21 Words and phrases

1 loads of **2** though **3** ability **4** nomadic people **5** victim **6** Persecution **7** attempt **8** forbade

22 Keywords

Mögliche Lösungen:

1 denied having **2** is forbidden **3** loads of things **4** pay attention **5** persuaded me to **6** at dawn **7** regret not buying **8** have an accident

23 Words and phrases

1 Holocaust **2** widespread **3** intention **4** refine **5** summarize **6** summary **7** proof of **8** corn **9** crop

24 Missing!

1 to/–/it **2** –/of/since **3** –/as/for **4** –/to/on **5** of/to/– **6** to/his/– **7** –/of/against **8** of/of/– **9** against/–/or **10** –/in/take **11** like/–/though **12** The/–/your

25 Words and phrases

1 12 acres **2** recently **3** shocking **4** propose **5** forward **6** from now **7** memorable **8** suffers from

26 The right word

1 memorable **2** suffer **3** shocking **4** summary **5** propose **6** acres/crops **7** ability **8** widespread **9** attempt **10** pass **11** riot **12** drew

27 Dialogues

Match the two parts of these dialogues.

1 This shop is quite expensive.
2 What do you call a bike for two?
3 Has he got a job?
4 I haven't run so far for years.
5 It's difficult to understand them. They speak so fast.
6 So, are you going to start cooking?
7 You said you go to the hub twice a week.
8 Imagine what it would be like to be a pilot.
9 My first job was to do the shop windows.
10 I have to adapt to the new team. I don't know any of them.
11 What do those statistics show?
12 Did you do chores when you were younger?

a Yes, you'd get to travel a lot!
b Don't worry. You'll get used to it.
c The percentage of refugees in each city.
d Yes, on average.
e Wow! That's a big responsibility.
f Yes, everything's handmade. That's why.
g Not really. He's a carer for his parents.
h I'm sure you'll fit in well.
i Well, I was supposed to.
j A tandem, I think.
k Sure. Where's the apron?
l I know, we're going to be stiff tomorrow.

28 Missing!

Complete these sentences by writing in the missing words or parts of words.

1 It's useful to know how to do ________ aid, in case something happens to someone.
2 Winter sports like skiing are ________ on the weather: they need snow.
3 He was absolutely ________broken when he couldn't go to the Olympics.
4 I don't buy much, but I love looking in shop ________ to see what there is.
5 ________fully everything will be finished soon so we can all go home early.
6 I travel everywhere by public ________port. It's not always quick, but it's cheap.
7 My dad's an ad____. His job is to en________ people to find solutions to their own problems.
8 They have different opinions on everything and never reach ________ment on anything.
9 I'm sure I don't need to re________ you how important good work is to this ________ation.
10 School is ________mally where young people form their most important friend________.

Big dreams – small steps

1 Words and phrases ➜ (pp. 58–59)

1 My brother is a soldier in the ________.	Mein Bruder ist Soldat in der **Armee**.
2 My sister is a good ________.	Meine Schwester ist eine gute **Athletin**.
3 Is ________ ________ the biggest problem today?	Ist die **Erderwärmung** das größte Problem heute?
4 Bike ________ __ ________ in cities.	Fahrräder **bewirken etwas** in Großstädten.
5 My grandpa used to ________ clocks.	Früher **reparierte** mein Opa Uhren.
6 We're doing a ________ experiment.	Wir machen ein **wissenschaftliches** Experiment.
7 I would like to try ________.	Ich würde gern **Fallschirmspringen** ausprobieren.
8 We've ________ a lot this year.	Wir **erreichten** in diesem Jahr viel.
9 It's important to have ________ in life.	Es ist wichtig, **Ziele** im Leben zu haben.
10 What's the ________ for our report?	Wann ist der **letzte Termin** für unseren Bericht?
11 He ________ to achieve his goal.	Er **scheiterte beim Versuch**, sein Ziel zu erreichen.
12 I sent my ________ yesterday.	Ich schickte gestern meine **Bewerbung**.
13 Lots of people ________ ____ the job.	Viele **bewarben sich um** die Stelle.

2 The right words

Choose the correct words from the box to complete these sentences. Not all the words are needed.

achieved · achieving · application · applications · applied · applying · army · athletes · deadline · difference · fail · failing · global warming · goal · goals · repaired · repairing · scientific · scientist · skydiving

1 Some people don't accept the ________ proof for ________ ________.

2 I'm thinking about ________ to join the ________.

3 One ________ of mine is to go ________.

4 The training made a ________ for the ________.

5 I ________ a lot today. I completed that job ________.

6 I ________ to understand why you didn't take the computer to be ________.

7 The ________ for ________ is next Friday.

3 Words and phrases ➔ (p. 60)

1 I read an ____________ from a novel in class.	Im Unterricht las ich einen **Auszug** aus einem Roman.
2 I'm the new ______-captain of the team.	Ich bin der neue **Vize**kapitän der Mannschaft.
3 We live in Bonn, the ____________ capital.	Wir wohnen in Bonn, der **ehemaligen** Hauptstadt.
4 Hurry up! The film is __________ ____ start.	Beeil dich! Der Film ist **kurz davor, zu** beginnen!
5 He spends hours on the basketball ________.	Er verbringt Stunden auf dem Basketball**spielfeld**.
6 They are twins and look ____________.	Sie sind Zwillinge und sehen **identisch** aus.
7 I first ___________ when I was 14.	Ich **rasierte mich** zum ersten Mal mit 14.
8 He's good , but he should ________ the ball more often.	Er ist gut, sollte aber den Ball häufiger **abspielen**.
9 I don't read the ________: I'm not ____________.	Ich lese die **Bibel** nicht: Ich bin nicht **religiös**.
10 My dad and my uncles are all _______.	Mein Vater und meine Onkel sind alle **glatzköpfig**.
11 Can you ______ what's wrong with the picture?	Kannst du **erkennen**, was mit dem Bild nicht stimmt?
12 I went red because it was so ________________.	Ich wurde rot, weil es so **peinlich** war.

4 Match the parts

Choose the right ending to complete the sentences.

1 I remembered my umbrella just when I was about
2 He gave us all a surprise when he came to school
3 In class we spent some time discussing an extract
4 I called the teacher the wrong name in class. It was
5 They were on the court practising how
6 I always find that time seems to pass very quickly
7 At the start of the lesson she gave me books to pass
8 You don't have to be religious to tell the difference
9 My mother has been made vice-president
10 The building is now offices, but it was a bank

a between right and wrong.
b really embarrassing.
c to pass the ball.
d with a shaved head.
e to lock the door.
f around the class.
g of the company.
h in former times.
i from the Bible.
j in the holidays.

5 Words and phrases ➜ (p. 61)

1 I ________ my clothes and put them on the bed.	Ich **faltete** meine Sachen und legte sie aufs Bett.
2 Mum always wears clothes that ________.	Mutti trägt immer Sachen, die **zusammenpassen**.
3 The ______ were caught in the ______.	Die **Fliegen** wurden im **Spinnennetz** gefangen.
4 He was told to ______ ______ his money.	Er wurde aufgefordert, sein Geld **auszuhändigen**.
5 The ______ was terrible in the tropics.	Die **Hitze** in den Tropen war furchtbar.
6 A cold ________ is often the sign that you are afraid.	Kalter **Schweiß** ist oft ein Zeichen von Angst.
7 I like ________ maths ______ French.	Ich mag **weder** Mathe **noch** Französisch.
8 Nobody likes people who ________.	Keiner mag Leute, die **schummeln**.
9 S______ it was such a nice day, we went for a walk.	**Da** es ein schöner Tag war, gingen wir spazieren.
10 The singer wore a skirt that was hardly ________.	Die Sängerin trug einen Rock, der kaum **anständig** war.
11 Is money the only thing that ________?	Ist Geld das einzige, was **wichtig ist**?
12 The ________ ________ in the building are very old.	Die **Wasserrohre** im Gebäude sind sehr alt.
13 They might ________ at any moment.	Sie könnten jeden Moment **platzen**.

6 Q&A

Match the two parts of these dialogues.

1 What matters most to you?
2 What's the easiest way of getting good results?
3 You look all wet. Have you been swimming?
4 I know this skirt is short, but do you like it?
5 Do you sometimes think Jane is a spider?
6 What do you want me to do with these clothes?
7 What do you think of my new socks and shoes?
8 Can you lend me a little money?
9 All their songs sound identical to me – do you agree?
10 We're not used to heat like this at this time of year, are we?
11 What happened when they told you to give them your money?
12 What's that noise? Is it a ghost!?

a Fold them and put them away.
b Well, it's decent – just!
c Well, similar anyway.
d Since it's you, OK.
e Well, I didn't hand it over. I ran!
f Well, it's not by cheating.
g No, this is sweat!
h That's global warming for you.
i Don't be silly. It's the water pipes.
j Yes, and Ken is a fly in her web.
k Friends and family, I guess.
l Nice. They match.

7 Words and phrases ➜ *(pp. 62–63)*

1 You've got a real ________ for languages.	Du hast ein echtes **Talent** für Sprachen.
2 Does ______________ always lead to success?	Führt **Intelligenz** immer zum Erfolg?
3 This pen was a ______ from my aunt.	Dieser Stift war ein **Geschenk** von meiner Tante.
4 Billy still believes in ________ ________.	Billy glaubt immer noch an den **Weihnachtsmann**.
5 I p________ an interesting book.	Ich **wählte** ein interessantes Buch **aus**.
6 The car didn't stop at the S__________.	Das Auto hielt nicht an der **Ampel**.
7 How would you describe your own ____________?	Wie würdest du deinen eigenen **Charakter** beschreiben?
8 She was hurt, but she was ________ and didn't cry.	Sie war verletzt, aber sie war **tapfer** und weinte nicht.
9 Sportspersons are normally _______________.	Sportler sind normalerweise **leistungsorientiert**.
10 My dad is _______ ________ old jazz music.	Mein Vater ist **verrückt nach** alter Jazzmusik.
11 Kim is a good friend. He's very ______.	Kim ist ein guter Freund. Er ist sehr **loyal**.
12 What were your ____________ before the test?	Was waren deine **Gefühle** vor dem Test?
13 Our teacher has a good _______ ___ ________.	Unser Lehrer hat **Humor**.
14 I think that's an important ________.	Ich denke, das ist eine wichtige **Eigenschaft**.

8 That's wrong!

Circle the mistake(s) in each line and write the correct word(s) on the right. Two lines are correct – which?

1 He always makes me laugh. He's got a great sens of houmor. ____________

2 Good atheletes want to win. They're very competetive. ____________

3 My favourite charakter in the extract was the brav girl. ____________

4 In sport tallent is more important than inteligence. ____________

5 It's embarassing to make the identic mistake twice. ____________

6 He's a very dezent person, even with people he disagrees with. ____________

7 I don't think you can achieve anything by cheating. ____________

8 He liked niether the heat or the flies in Australia. ____________

9 One of the baskets on the cort needs to be repared. ____________

10 Your honest opinion really matters to us, said the vice-president. ____________

9 Words and phrases ➜ *(pp. 63–64)*

1 There's a ______________ shop I like very much.	Es gibt einen **bestimmten** Laden, den ich sehr mag.
2 He was very ____________ with his time.	Er war mit seiner Zeit sehr **großzügig**.
3 I'm __________________, but you are ______.	Ich bin **fleißig**, aber du bist **faul**.
4 It was very ________ of you to say that.	Es war sehr **gemein** von dir, das zu sagen.
5 You have to be ____________ ____ others.	Man muss **tolerant gegenüber** anderen sein.
6 You can use ____________ to make new words.	Man verwendet **Nachsilben**, um neue Wörter zu bilden.
7 These are words of ____________ meaning.	Das sind Wörter **entgegengesetzter** Bedeutung.
8 I don't _____________ this place. Where are we?	Ich **erkenne** diesen Ort nicht. Wo sind wir?
9 I never make ________________ about exams.	Ich mache nie **Voraussagen** zu Prüfungen.
10 Roads are divided into different _____________.	Straßen werden in verschiedene **Kategorien** unterteilt.
11 I enjoy ____________ and I love _________.	Ich genieße **Kanufahren** und ich mag **Lyrik** sehr.

10 Three into one

Join the three parts (one from each column) to make sentences.

1 There's no	a crazy	I salary, but we work hard for it.
2 Yesterday I had a	b brave	II supporter of the local team.
3 Not everyone is as	c scientific	III situation that I went bright red.
4 We get a very	d lazy	IV of you to go skydiving.
5 I come from a	e religious	V family where we all have two jobs.
6 My brother was very	f particular	VI evening watching TV at home.
7 Gabriella has always been a	g generous	VII methods to find criminals.
8 I think it was very	h hard-working	VIII to me when we were young.
9 Everyone in my family is	i tolerant	IX reason I don't like him. I just don't.
10 Different people have different	j loyal	X of people's differences as you, unfortunately.
11 The police use	k mean	XI about watersports, especially canoeing.
12 I found it such an	l embarrassing	XII beliefs. That's life.

11 Words and phrases ➜ (p. 66)

1 Do you like doing scientific ______________?	Macht ihr gern naturwissenschaftliche **Experimente**?
2 I was ill with a ________ when I was on holiday.	Ich erkrankte mit einem **Virus**, als ich im Urlaub war.
3 She's trying to ______________ the illness.	Sie versucht, die Krankheit zu **diagnostizieren**.
4 _____ _________ I have, _____ __________ I am.	**Je mehr** ich habe, **desto glücklicher** bin ich.
5 Can you imagine life before ______________?	Kannst du dir ein Leben ohne **Kühlung** vorstellen?
6 Scientists spend lots of time in the _____.	Wissenschaftler verbringen viel Zeit im **Labor**.
7 I want to work for an international ___________.	Ich will für eine internationale **Firma** arbeiten.
8 He ___________ to work at the weekend.	Er **weigerte sich**, am Wochenende zu arbeiten.
9 I need these ______________ for my experiment.	Ich brauche diese **Chemikalien** für mein Projekt.
10 We arrived ___ ________ _____ the start of the match.	Wir kamen **rechtzeitig zu** dem Anfang des Spieles an.

12 Almost the same

Match the sentences with similar meanings.

1 I asked him but he said no and that was that.
2 He said he needed it as quickly as possible.
3 He promised he wouldn't be late.
4 He's really hard-working.
5 He says everyone is different and you have to accept it.
6 He looks completely different these days.
7 His kitchen has flooded.
8 He always makes me laugh.
9 He's very generous. He gave it to me.
10 He was the one who chose the restaurant.
11 He runs his own company.
12 He spends all his money on travel.

a You certainly couldn't call him lazy.
b I nearly didn't recognise him.
c He's crazy about it.
d He picked where to eat.
e He said he'd be there in time.
f It was a gift.
g He simply refused.
h He's got a great sense of humour.
i He's very tolerant.
j He said the sooner, the better.
k His water pipes have burst.
l He has no boss.

13 Words and phrases → (p. 66)

1 She likes sport but her real __________ is music.	Sie mag Sport, aber ihre echte **Leidenschaft** ist die Musik.
2 The idea ______________ into a big project.	Die Idee **entwickelte sich** zu einem großen Projekt.
3 Her __________ boyfriend is called John.	Ihr **aktueller** Freund heißt John.
4 I have to __________ my work ____ my teacher.	Ich muss die Arbeit **bei** meinem Lehrer **einreichen**.
5 A book ______ takes place in Frankfurt every year.	Eine Buch**messe** findet jedes Jahr in Frankfurt statt.
6 The price ____________ travel and hotel costs.	Der Preis **beinhaltet** Reise- und Hotelkosten.
7 I want to study _____________ at university.	Ich will an der Uni **Medizin** studieren.
8 Modern cities _______ ____ Berlin are really cool.	Moderne Städte **wie etwa** Berlin sind echt cool.
9 Without _______________ you achieve nothing.	Ohne **Motivation** erreicht man nichts.

14 Quiz time!

1 What are "-ness", "-ity" and "-ence" at the end of words? ____________________

2 What do you call someone who has no hair? ____________________

3 Young children think this person brings them gifts in December. ____________________

4 The hobby of jumping out of a plane. ____________________

5 The opposite of accept. ____________________

6 The second-most important person after the president of a company. ____________________

7 If you get a bad result in a test. ____________________

8 What's the fourth word? Swimming: pool, basketball: … ____________________

9 What people who want to be doctors study. ____________________

10 The liquid your body produces when it is very hot. ____________________

11 Something you say about what you think will happen in the future. ____________________

12 Ebola is an example. ____________________

13 Love and hate are examples. ____________________

14 Where can scientists work? ____________________

15 Words and phrases ➜ *(p. 67)*

1 My sister used to have a ________ as a pet.	Meine Schwester hatte früher eine **Maus** als Haustier.
2 Animals change over time. That's __________.	Tiere ändern sich mit der Zeit. Das heißt **Evolution**.
3 So, how are you going to ________ the problem?	So, wie wirst du das Problem **in Angriff nehmen**?
4 What are you doing in _________ this week?	Was macht ihr diese Woche in **Biologie**?
5 There's an _______ number of boys and girls.	Es gibt die **gleiche** Zahl von Jungen und Mädchen.
6 Bears don't feel cold; their _____ is very _______.	Bären wird es nicht kalt; ihr **Fell** ist sehr **dick**.
7 We will find the answer. This isn't a _______ _______.	Wir finden die Antwort. Das ist keine **Sackgasse**.
8 The lab is closed. They're ________ it _________.	Das Labor hat zu. Sie **lassen** es **streichen**.
9 This is no problem ____ _____ ______ ______.	Das ist **langfristig** kein Problem.
10 You show a good _________________ of the topic.	Du zeigst ein gutes **Verständnis** vom Thema.

16 One from two

Decide which word completes the sentence.

1 It's more than a hobby for me. It's an absolute	**a** biology
2 We will all see the advantages of this in the long	**b** fair
3 We learn about nature and how the body works in	**c** evolution
4 Species have changed over time. That's	**d** fur
5 I don't like to eat foods that have been grown using	**e** term
6 I went to talk to a lot of different companies at the job	**f** mouse
7 The work we did wasn't useful. We went down a blind	**g** passion
8 I don't think people should wear clothes made from	**h** motivation
9 For the scientific experiment they used a white	**i** chemicals
10 You won't get anywhere in life or sport without	**j** alley

17 Words and phrases ➜ *(pp. 67–70)*

1 I understand the ____________ of evolution now.	Ich verstehe jetzt das **Prinzip** der Evolution.
2 I ____ think exam results are important.	Ich glaube **wirklich**, dass Prüfungsergebnisse wichtig sind.
3 Some people will do anything to __________.	Manche machen alles, um **Erfolg** zu **haben**.
4 The result will be ______________ tomorrow.	Das Ergebnis wird morgen **bekanntgegeben**.
5 I don't plan. I like to be ________________.	Ich plane nicht. Ich bin gern **spontan**.
6 When I was young, I loved ________ stories.	Als ich jung war, mochte ich **Piraten**geschichten sehr.
7 This chapter __________ on evolution.	Dieses Kapitel **konzentriert sich** auf die Evolution.
8 The police ___________ the area for clues.	Die Polizei **durchsuchte** das Gebiet nach Hinweisen.
9 You should ______ your work every 10 minutes.	Man sollte seine Arbeit alle 10 Minuten **speichern**.

18 Missing!

Add words to two of the three gaps in each line.

1 Having relevant ______ experience makes ______ huge difference when ______ comes to applying for jobs.

2 I need ______ money so I want to find a job, and ______ sooner ______ better.

3 ______ languages ______ as English and Spanish ______ spoken all over the world.

4 I don't know why my sister wants to be ______ doctor. ______ Mum nor Dad are in ______ medicine.

5 It's important to ______ spontaneous, but in the ______ term, success comes from ______ planning.

6 You might not think ______, but I really ______ want your project to ______ succeed.

7 My hair is in ______ eyes. It's ______ too long now. I think I'll ______ it cut at the weekend.

8 Before I book a holiday, I want ______ know ______ exactly what's ______ in the price.

9 Dad is often away with his ______ business, but he always comes back ______ time ______ Christmas.

10 In addition to ______ good understanding of people, you need ______ a good sense ______ humour in this job.

19 Words and phrases ➜ (pp. 70–72)

1 I ______ myself ____ an hour of TV a day.	Ich **begrenze** mich **auf** 1 Stunde TV pro Tag.
2 Think ______ before you give the answer.	Überlege **sorgfältig**, bevor du die Antwort gibst.
3 The Italians ______ a lot of wine.	Die Italiener **stellen** viel Wein **her**.
4 What's the ______ of your information?	Wie lautet die **Quelle** deiner Informationen?
5 I won't go ______ you go too.	Ich gehe nicht, **außer** du gehst auch.
6 She ______ Shakespeare in her work.	Sie **zitierte** Shakespeare in ihrer Arbeit.
7 These are English ______ ______: "…"	Das sind deutsche **Anführungszeichen**: „…"
8 He uses a lot of ______ when he speaks.	Er verwendet beim Reden viele **Handbewegungen**.
9 Does your football team have a ______?	Hat dein Fußballverein ein **Maskottchen**?
10 I'm planning to run a ______ this year.	Ich plane, dieses Jahr **Marathon** zu laufen.

20 Scrambled report

Put the parts in the correct order. The first one has been done for you.

a People say it's important to aim high in life and work hard to

c the ball after school and when we are playing another team in a school

b in a band. As for me, what I want more than anything else is to be

n to me. My friends tell me I have the right qualities: neither motivation

d favourite is basketball. I feel completely at home when I am on the

g as wanting to start their own business, or to be a film star and work

h dreams come true it's better to take small steps than to expect to

f in Hollywood. Another of my friends from school just wants to play

i nor hard work are a problem for me. Things are going well now. To

l succeed immediately. Some of my friends have ambitions such

m court, both when we are practising something like passing

j date we have won all our matches, and that has increased our confidence

o competition. I am quite competitive, and winning really matters

k a professional basketball player. All sports are great, but my particular

e achieve your goals, which makes sense. They also say to make big

Answer: a ☐ ☐ ☐ ☐ ☐ ☐ ☐ ☐ ☐ ☐ ☐ ☐ ☐ ☐

21 Words and phrases ➔ *(p. 72)*

1 Your button needs to be ______ back on.	Dein Knopf muss wieder an**genäht** werden.
2 I want a job where I can be __________.	Ich will eine Arbeit, bei der **kreativ** sein kann.
3 I'll do it. You can ______ ____ me.	Ich mache es. Du kannst **dich auf** mich **verlassen**.
4 Please __________ us for more details.	**Melden Sie sich** bitte **bei** uns, um Näheres zu erfahren.
5 Lots of houses were ____________ in the storm.	Viele Häuser wurden im Unwetter **beschädigt**.
6 His money is in a _______ until he's 18.	Sein Geld ist in einer **Stiftung**, bis er 18 wird.
7 My uncle ___________ old cars.	Mein Onkel **restauriert** alte Autos.

22 Fill the gaps

Use one word from each of two boxes (**A + B**, **A + C**, or **B + C**) to complete each of these sentences.

A
do • focus • gesture • rely • tell • unless

B
not • on • principles • refused • restored • science • too

C
again • carefully • lab • on • since • marathon • work

1 Young children ____________ ____________ their parents for everything. That's natural.

2 They're having the chairs and sofas ____________ so they can use them ____________.

3 I couldn't run a ____________; it's just ____________ far for me.

4 This year I need to ____________ ____________ getting the best possible exam results.

5 Our ____________ lessons are normally in the ____________.

6 You can ____________ when someone is competitive from the way they ____________.

7 I'm ____________ going to tell you ____________ you ask.

8 Let me know if you ____________ decide to go ____________ I've heard the film is worth seeing.

9 I'm going to explain the ____________ of the trust , so listen ____________.

10 The police officer made a ____________ at the driver to stop but the driver ____________.

23 Words and phrases ➔ *(pp. 72–73)*

1 How many ______________ were there for the job?	Wie viele **Bewerber** gab es auf die Stelle?
2 This is my first ____ in English.	Das ist mein erster **Lebenslauf** auf Englisch.
3 How much ____________ information is necessary?	Wie viele **persönliche** Informationen sind nötig?
4 What do I say in a ____________ ______________?	Was schreibe ich in einem **Motivationsschreiben**?
5 The president made a ______________ on the radio.	Die Präsidentin gab eine **Erklärung** im Radio ab.
6 Which ______________ will you vote for?	Für welchen **Kandidaten** wirst du stimmen?
7 Give the ________ of your work experience.	Gib die **Daten** deiner Arbeitserfahrung an.
8 Put them in __________ order.	Gib sie in **umgekehrter** Reihenfolge an.
9 The book uses ________ I don't understand.	Das Buch verwendet **Begriffe**, die ich nicht verstehe.
10 Have you had this CV ______________?	Hast du diesen Lebenslauf **Korrektur lesen** lassen?
11 Where in this ____________________ do you live?	Wo in diesem **Viertel** wohnst du?
12 It's expensive! Prices have _____________ a lot.	Es ist teuer. Die Preise **sind** sehr **gestiegen**.

24 A conversation about CVs

Put the replies in this dialogue in the correct order.

1 What are the most important things to include in a CV? I've never written one before.

2 So should I include all the exams I passed and failed from primary school?

3 Right. And do I put in details of the hobbies I enjoy?

4 What about things such as relaxing, watching TV and playing video games?

5 You mean, a sentence or two to show I'm someone with motivation and qualities like that?

6 Right, so I shouldn't make things up, you mean?

7 Finally, what sort of experience do you think is important to include?

a I'd leave them out, to be honest. And you need to write a personal statement.

b Yes, especially things like team sports because that could be releavant to the jobs you want.

c Absolutely. You wouldn't cheat in an exam, so you must also stick to the truth on your CV.

d Well, if you've been a volunteer, or looked after children – things that show you are a responsible person.

e No, I'd focus on secondary school. And just put the main ones, like the *Abitur*, of course.

f Exactly. But make sure they are true because if you have an interview they will ask you about that.

g Well, start with your education and the subjects you studied at school, and your qualifications.

25 Words and phrases ➔ (p. 73)

1 You need a ______________ of biology to be a doctor.	Du brauchst Biologie**kenntnisse**, um Arzt zu werden.
2 We've sold over 2,000 books ____ ______.	Wir haben **bis heute** über 2.000 Bücher verkauft.
3 Are you already at ______________ ________?	Besuchst du schon die **weiterführende Schule**?
4 Or do you still go to ____________ __________?	Oder bist du noch an der **Grundschule**?
5 Did you get a ________________ from the course?	Hast du vom Kurs eine **Qualifikation** bekommen?
6 I like sewing and ______ ________.	Ich mag Nähen und **Filzen**.
7 On ______________ of the course I soon found a job.	Nach **Abschluss** des Kurses fand ich bald eine Stelle.
8 Lots of young people want to work in ___.	Viele junge Leute woll in der **IT** arbeiten.
9 I'm reading a book about _________ history.	Ich lese ein Buch über die **römische** Geschichte.

26 The right word

Circle the correct word to complete the sentences.

1 We got a qualification on **complete • completed • completion** of the course.

2 The quality of the **applied • applicants • application** was really high.

3 I don't know very much about **Rome • Roman • Romanish** architecture.

4 Her **knowledge • knowing • know** of biology is very impressive.

5 I've never **sewn • sewing • sew** a button on a shirt before.

6 These are his words, so put them in **quotation • quote • quoted** marks.

7 I made a **spontan • spontaning • spontaneous** decision to walk into the cinema.

8 Because she reacted quickly, she managed to **safe • save • saved** his life.

9 My dream job would be one where I can be **create • creative • creating** .

10 I don't like having to rely **in • on • with** other people.

11 Be calm. Don't let your **quality • emotion • talent** control how you think.

12 I spent hours **proofreading • proofingread • proofingreading** my CV.

13 What's your **person • personal • personally** opinion about cheating?

14 Animals are protected from the cold by their **big • fat • thick** fur.

27 Keywords

Rewrite the sentences using the keywords so they mean the same as the original. Don't change the keyword in any way.

1 There were hundreds of applicants for the job. applied

Many people ______________________________.

2 I only allow the children to use the computer for an hour a day at the weekend. limit

At weekends, I ______________________________ on the computer.

3 He'll only eat meat if he knows where it comes from. unless

He refuses ______________________________ where it's from.

4 If you don't want to fail in life, you have to work hard. succeed

The only way ______________________________ work hard.

5 I don't like canoeing and I don't like poetry. nor

I like ______________________________.

6 We have ten girls and ten boys in our class. equal

There's ______________________________ boys and girls in our class.

7 I got someone to repair my computer for me. had

When my computer stopped working I ______________________________.

8 Many people have died because of things like the Ebola virus. as

Illnesses ______________________________ have killed many people.

9 We have to submit our project on Friday or before. deadline

Friday ______________________________ the project.

28 Missing!

Complete these sentences by writing in the missing words or parts of words.

1 His know__________ of the basic princ__________ of refrig__________ is impressive. He's an expert.

2 My pers__________ ambition is to run a mara__________ this year.

3 I didn't really enjoy prim__________ school, but __________ school was great.

4 The number of young families moving into this neigh__________ has in__________ a lot.

5 He made a __________ment about the value and contri__________ of the team mas__________.

6 He loves re__________ that old car so much that he won't set a dead__________ for finishing.

4 Unit

It's up to you

1 Words and phrases ➜ *(pp. 82–83)*

1 She can go if she wants. ____ ____ ____ her.	Sie kann gehen, wenn sie will. Sie **hat die Wahl**.
2 We are learning lots about the __________.	Wir lernen gerade viel über die **Antarktis**.
3 The people ______ ____ and protested.	Die Leute **erhoben sich** und protestierten.
4 __________ action is the best way to win.	Eine **vereinte** Aktion ist die beste Art zu siegen.
5 I ______ every day because it's healthy.	Ich **fahre** jeden Tag **mit dem Rad**, da es gesund ist.
6 They _________ ______ the end of the war.	Sie **führten** das Ende des Krieges **herbei**.
7 How can we start this _________?	Wie können wir diese **Initiative** anfangen?
8 We asked them to _____ our ________.	Wir baten sie, unsere **Petition** zu **unterschreiben**.
9 The school is closed because of the ______.	Die Schule ist wegen des **Sitzstreiks** geschlossen.
10 There was a _______ through town yesterday.	Gestern gab es einen **Marsch** durch die Stadt.
11 The workers are planning to ____ ____ ______.	Die Arbeiter haben vor, **in den Streik** zu **treten**.
12 We should ________ that company's ________.	Wir sollten die **Produkte** der Firma **boykottieren**.

2 The right words

Choose the correct words from the box to complete these sentences.

> Antarctic · boycott · bring · about · collective · cycle · initiative · marches · on strike · petition · products · sign · sit-in · up · you

1 They asked me to ________ their ________ but I didn't.

2 We should ________ the ________ the company makes.

3 I've been on several ________, but the ________ in the library was my first.

4 If you want to ________ change, then ________ more and use cars less.

5 The decision to go ________ was a ________ one.

6 I read about the new ________ to prevent pollution in the ________.

7 You don't have to come with us if you don't want. It's ________ to ________.

3 Words and phrases ➜ *(pp. 84–86)*

1 What is your opinion of the __________ __________?	Was ist deine Meinung zu den **Vereinten Nationen**?
2 A ______________ takes place here every year.	Ein **Kongress** findet hier jedes Jahr statt.
3 Traffic near schools needs to be _________ ______.	Der Verkehr vor Schulen muss **verlangsamt** werden.
4 The ______________ was __________ by the artist.	Die **Installation** wurde vom Künstler **erschaffen**.
5 We ____________ our film on the wall.	Wir **projizierten** unseren Film an die Wand.
6 ____ ____ __ ________ someone called my name.	**Plötzlich** rief jemand meinen Namen.
7 I haven't seen him in the ______ year.	Ich habe ihn im **letzten** Jahr nicht gesehen.
8 What ___________ tense did the ___________ use?	Welches **Erzähl**tempus verwendete der **Erzähler**?
9 The event is ___ __________ now.	Das Ereignis ist jetzt **im Gange**.
10 The ______ of the mountain took his breath away.	Der **Anblick** des Berges verschlug ihm den Atem.
11 It's dark ____ _____ ______ he gets home in the winter.	Es ist dunkel, **wenn** er im Winter nach Hause kommt.
12 We _____ ________ a 10-minute _______.	Wir **machen** eine zehnminütige **Pause**.

4 Logic!

Match the two parts of these dialogues logically.

1 Where does his dad work?
2 You can't go in there now.
3 I like that installation.
4 Are those dogs actually barking to music?
5 I'm pretty tired, actually.
6 She's not seeing Mark now, is she?
7 Many accidents are caused by people driving too fast.
8 I can't find the screen anywhere.
9 Why did he give all those details about the weather?
10 I'd really like to go to a conference.

a Do you think he was setting the scene?
b OK, do you want to take a break?
c No, that's all in the past, isn't it?
d Think so. Quite a sight, isn't it?
e Yes. Who created it?
f Why? Is there a meeting in progress?
g Why are you interested in politics all of a sudden?
h Is it the United Nations?
i Why don't we project on the wall, then?
j So what's the best way to slow them down?

5 Words and phrases ➔ *(p. 87)*

1 How would you ____________ this picture?	Wie würdest du dieses Bild **deuten**?
2 This glass ___________ exactly 543 ml.	Dieses Glas **enthält** genau 543 ml.
3 Are you _____________ ________ racism?	Bist du **besorgt über** Rassismus?
4 The painter __________ city life beautifully.	Der Maler **stellt** das Stadtleben schön **dar**.
5 He _____________ ____ urban problems.	Er **äußert sich zu** städtischen Problemen.
6 How would you __________ this news?	Wie würest du diese Nachricht **analysieren**?
7 __________________ problems are ___________.	**Umwelt**probleme sind **politische** Probleme.
8 The party __________ ____ poor people.	Die Partei **lenkt den Blick auf** arme Leute.
9 She took a photo of a _________.	Sie machte ein Foto von einem **Kaktus**.
10 This is an ____________ way of solving the problem.	Das ist eine **wirkungsvolle** Art, das Problem zu lösen.
11 The film really _______ me think.	Der Film **brachte** mich wirklich **zum** Nachdenken.
12 I'm not going to _______ you visit Granny.	Ich werde dich nicht **zwingen**, Oma **zu** besuchen.
13 The message ________ ________ very clearly.	Die Botschaft **kommt** sehr deutlich **rüber**.

6 Missing!

Complete the words with the missing letters.

1 Pollution is definitely a major _ _ **v i** _ _ _ _ _ _ _ _ _ problem in the country now.

2 Do you have any strong _ _ **l i** _ _ _ _ _ views on this subject?

3 How would you _ _ **t e r** _ _ _ _ _ his behaviour?

4 He wrote a first person _ _ _ **r a** _ _ _ _ about the march he went on.

5 What's the most _ _ **f e** _ _ _ _ _ way of bringing about change, in your opinion?

6 The cartoon is _ _ _ **m e n** _ _ _ _ on the causes of global warming.

7 Every year they have a _ _ _ **f e r** _ _ _ _ in a city like London or Birmingham.

8 If you _ _ **y c** _ _ _ a country or company, they earn less money.

9 The cost of food is something that I am very _ _ **n c** _ _ _ _ _ about.

10 The poster _ _ **n t** _ _ _ _ a simple message: you are what you eat.

7 Words and phrases ➜ (pp. 39–42)

1 Will you ______ ___ ________ ____ this problem?	Wirst du **zu** diesem Problem **Stellung beziehen**?
2 This is a ________ to peace.	Dies ist eine **Bedrohung** für den Frieden.
3 I received an ______________ letter.	Ich erhielt einen **anonymen** Brief.
4 The ________ ___________ discussed this issue.	Die **Premierministerin** besprach das Thema.
5 Two _____________ are working on the problem.	Zwei **Ministerien** arbeiten an dem Problem.
6 I'm against the ____________ of wildlife.	Ich bin gegen das **Abschlachten** frei lebender Tiere.
7 She faced the _______ of the students.	Sie wurde mit dem **Zorn** der Studenten konfrontiert.
8 The storm is now _____ _____ _______ of Scotland.	Das Gewitter ist jetzt **vor der Küste** Schottlands.
9 We went swimming in a beautiful ______.	Wir gingen in einer schönen **Bucht** schwimmen.
10 We'll go ________ tomorrow ___ the next day.	Wir gehen **entweder** morgen **oder** übermorgen.
11 To sell _________ you need a ________.	Um **Alkohol** zu verkaufen, braucht man eine **Lizenz**.
12 We're starting a ____________ at school.	Wir starten eine **Kampagne** in der Schule an.
13 I read about the ______ the ________ received.	Ich las von der **Geldstrafe**, die der **Besitzer** erhielt.
14 The __________ ended as a ____________ died.	Die **Versammlung** endete, als eine **Stadträtin** starb.

8 That's wrong!

Circle the two mistakes in each line and write the correct words on the right. One line is correct – which?

1 I received an anonym treat by email. It was frightening. ____________________

2 We could go to the coaste or on Monday or on Friday. ____________________

3 We need to take a standing on the slaugter of animals. ____________________

4 The counciller talked about the problems caused by alcool. ____________________

5 The ownor has applied for a lisense to sell wine and beer. ____________________

6 The mayor gave some thought to the issues from the meeting. ____________________

7 The message of the campaing came accross well. ____________________

8 Creating extra work will result in the wroth of all the ministeries. ____________________

9 She wanted to focuss on different ways to interprete the message. ____________________

10 They hackered the website, which made me worrying a lot. ____________________

9 Words and phrases ➔ (pp. 88–89)

1 I saw you there. You can't ________ it.	Ich sah dich da. Du kannst es nicht **bestreiten**.
2 The government ________ the new law.	Die Regierung **verabschiedete** das neue Gesetz.
3 If you drive like that, you ________ a fine.	Wenn du so fährst, **riskierst** du eine Geldstrafe.
4 I don't ________ ________ the idea that fashion is fun.	Ich **glaube** nicht an die Idee, dass Mode Spaß macht.
5 It is a ________ that life used to be better.	Es ist ein **Mythos**, dass das Leben früher besser war.
6 What ________ is your dog?	Welches **Geschlecht** hat dein Hund?
7 Do you believe in racial ________?	Glaubst du an die **Gleichheit** der Rassen?
8 In ________ men get better ________.	In der **Wirklichkeit** bekommen Männer mehr **Lohn**.
9 We're concerned about the ________ of our kids.	Wir sind besorgt wegen der Sicherheit unserer **Kinder**.
10 He nearly had an ________ here yesterday.	Er hatte hier gestern fast einen **Unfall**.
11 We're doing a ________ on modern music.	Wir machen eine **Umfrage** zu moderner Musik.

10 Three into one

Join the three parts (one from each column) to make sentences.

1 Business owners are often cautious, but I know some who have	a made	I the people in the cove so naturally.
2 The security of the website was a priority, which is why it hasn't been	b bought	II any involvement in the crime.
3 I think it is very impressive that the artist has	c given	III quickly and soon they had to go home.
4 The advert was so effective that it	d risked	IV at all since the company began.
5 Gender equality is simply not a reality yet and I have never	e denied	V the scene nicely.
6 Perhaps because they were having such a great time the hours	f set	VI a lot of thought to preparing the presentation.
7 Discrimination is one of the few things that my brother has actively	g depicted	VII everything in order to succeed.
8 The man the police arrested last night	h hacked	VIII into the myth that it does.
9 The results show that she has	i taken	IX a stand on, in fact.
10 Giving details about where the story took place	j passed	X me want to buy some immediately.

11 Words and phrases ➔ *(pp. 89–90)*

1 We're going to write to our local _____.	Wir schreiben unserem örtlichen **MdB**.
2 We want to _____ _____ to change this.	Wir wollen **tätig werden**, um dies zu ändern.
3 You have to _____ it's not going to be easy.	Man muss **zugeben**, dass es nicht einfach sein wird.
4 The competition ___ ___ take place tomorrow.	Das Wettbewerb **soll** morgen stattfinden.
5 They say there's a _____ ___ every problem.	Man sagt, **für** jedes Problem gibt es eine **Lösung**.
6 I'm _____ going to do my best.	Ich werde **auf jeden Fall** mein Bestes geben.
7 You should _____ all the choices first.	Du solltest zuerst alle Optionen **berücksichtigen**.
8 He _____ _____ a new car.	Er **zog in Betracht**, ein neues Auto zu **kaufen**.
9 Cars _____ ___ more space than bikes.	Autos **beanspruchen** mehr Platz als Fahrräder.
10 Put your _____ on before you get on the bike.	Setz dein **Helm** auf, bevor du aufs Fahrrad steigst.
11 If you want to eat, I ___ _____ ___ cook.	Wenn du essen willst, koche ich **gerne**.

12 Almost the same

Match the sentences with similar meanings.

1 That's no problem.
2 It takes up too much space.
3 I finally found the answer.
4 Yes, I admit it.
5 I'm thinking about it.
6 I'm going to do something about it.
7 Things are not like that, in my opinion.
8 I asked a lot of people what they thought.
9 A lot of people think like that, but I don't agree.
10 I'd hate to be a politician.
11 They're going to pass a law against that.
12 The answer came to me in the end.

a I can't deny it.
b I'm going to take action.
c I did a survey on it.
d I'm happy to help.
e I haven't got enough room.
f I finally found an effective solution.
g I would never be an MP.
h It's something I'm considering.
i I got the solution in the end.
j I think that's a myth.
k I don't buy into that.
l I think it's going to be illegal soon.

13 Words and phrases ➜ *(pp. 91–92)*

1 The storm has ____________ the bridge.	Der Sturm **schwächte** die Brücke.
2 Strong arguments are better than ________ ones.	Starke Argumente sind besser als **schwache**.
3 Do you think all animals feel ______?	Meinst du, dass alle Tiere **Schmerz** empfinden?
4 I ________ my voice but I didn't shout.	Ich **erhob** meine Stimme aber schrie nicht.
5 My grandmother ________ six children.	Meine Großmutter **zog** sechs Kinder **groß**.
6 The film ________ the question of equality.	Der Film **bringt** das Thema der Gleichheit **zur Sprache**.
7 ____ you ______ _____ pizza tonight?	**Hast** du heute Abend **Lust auf** Pizza?
8 Not really, I ______ ______ _______ to the cinema.	Eigentlich nicht, ich **habe Lust**, ins Kino zu **gehen**.
9 I said something I ____________ later.	Ich sagte etwas, was ich später **bereute**.
10 I ________ not __________ earlier.	Ich **bedauere**, nicht früher **angefangen zu haben**.
11 We did____ go __________ last weekend.	Wir sind letztes Wochenende **nirgendwohin** gefahren.
12 This plant is _____ found ___________ else.	Diese Pflanze wird **nirgendwo** anders gefunden.
13 10,000 people ____________ the plan.	10.000 Leute **protestierten gegen** den Plan.
14 Fortunately it wasn't a problem _______ ____.	Glücklicherweise war es **doch** kein Problem.

14 Quiz time!

1 You wear this to protect your head when you cycle. ____________________

2 What's the fourth word: accept – reject, admit – … ____________________

3 This plant is often found in the desert. ____________________

4 The feeling when you are angry. ____________________

5 When you wish you hadn't done something. ____________________

6 You can do this to children, your voice and questions. ____________________

7 When a writer doesn't put his or her name, a text is … ____________________

8 In the UK, this person is the most important MP. ____________________

9 What people do when they march or have a sit-in. ____________________

10 The opposite of danger. ____________________

15 Words and phrases ➔ *(p. 93)*

1 His ________ in politics is important to him.	Sein **Engagement** für die Politik ist ihm wichtig.
2 She ___ ______ very ______ in the theatre.	Sie **engagiert sich** gerade sehr am Theater.
3 The ______ was an ______ as a student.	Der **Senator** war als Student **Aktivist**.
4 Do you think ______ works well?	Meinst du, dass **Aktivismus** gut funktioniert?
5 Grandpa worries about ________.	Opa macht sich Sorgen wegen der **Einwanderung**.
6 He was born in Wales but is a German ______.	Er kommt aus Wales, ist aber deutscher **Staatsbürger**.
7 He's going to a big ______ in London.	Er geht auf einen großen **Kongress** in London.
8 In a ______, we all have a vote.	In einer **Demokratie** haben wir alle eine Stimme.
9 Thousands ________ against the war.	Tausend **demonstrierten** gegen den Krieg.
10 It's illegal to ________ ______ people.	Es ist illegal, Leute zu **diskriminieren**.

16 One from two

Decide which word completes the sentence.

1 I didn't think he was interested in politics. It was a surprise to read about his	**a** activist.
2 You can criticize the government. That's how things work in a	**b** citizen.
3 He's very ambitious and would really like to become a	**c** voices.
4 Every weekend she's protesting on a march somewhere. She's a real	**d** reality.
5 She was born in Japan, but she's now an American	**e** congress.
6 I like the film because it raises an important	**f** accident.
7 We could tell from the noise that the animal was definitely in	**g** involvement.
8 It was very loud because everyone was talking in raised	**h** democracy.
9 The government is spending a lot to improve the local	**i** senator.
10 Each year they have a vote to decide who to send to the	**j** infrastructure.
11 You can talk about equal pay, but that's still not the	**k** question.
12 The road was closed as a result of the	**l** pain.

17 Words and phrases ➔ *(pp. 96–97)*

1 This film ___ ________ ___ real events.	Dieser Film **basiert auf** wahren Ereignissen.
2 Most people want to ________ war.	Die meisten wollen dem Krieg **entkommen**.
3 Many news stories are about ________.	In vielen Nachrichten geht es um **Gewalt**.
4 My parents always get up at ______.	Meine Eltern stehen immer bei **Sonnenaufgang** auf.
5 We ________ round the table for a chat.	Wir **versammelten uns** um den Tisch, um zu plaudern.
6 I won't forget what I saw. It was ________.	Ich vergesse nie, was ich sah. Es war **grauenhaft**.
7 He ________ when the police arrested him.	Er **wehrte sich**, als die Polizei ihn verhaftete.
8 He ate breakfast in his ________.	Er aß sein Frühstück im **Schlafanzug**.
9 I ______ an ______ yesterday.	Ich **legte** gestern eine **Prüfung ab**.
10 I can't hear you. The _____ is awful.	Ich höre dich nicht. Die **Leitung** ist schrecklich.
11 There will be an ________ against the decision.	Es wird eine **Berufung** gegen die Entscheidung geben.
12 The main ________ is _____ more pay.	Die Haupt**forderung** ist **nach** mehr Lohn.
13 We could march to the ______ ______.	Wir könnten zum **Innenministerium** marschieren.
14 My mother works in the English ________.	Meine Mutter arbeitet im **Fachbereich** Englisch.

18 The right word

Circle the correct word to complete the sentences.

1 He called the doctor because he was **in • on • under** pain.

2 I don't like fiction. I prefer things based **about • from • on** real events.

3 I don't think marches and sit-ins ever bring **on • back • about** real change.

4 He said he wanted to see the film, but he didn't go **after • later • last** all.

5 My grandparents loved the village and wouldn't live anywhere **other • else • more** .

6 It can't continue like this. We're going to take **act • action • acting** .

7 I've got to focus **on • in • with** my exams, this year.

8 This bed is too big. It takes **in • over • up** too much space in the room.

9 The factory is closed because the workers are **in • on • off** strike.

10 The president is **for • going • to** open the new university tomorrow.

19 Words and phrases ➜ (p. 97)

1 The children are all in the ________________.	Die Kinder sind alle auf dem **Spielplatz**.
2 What's that noise? It sounds like a ______.	Was ist der Lärm? Es klingt wie ein **Aufstand**.
3 Over 2 million died in the US ______ ______.	Mehr als 2 Millionen starben im **Bürgerkrieg** der USA.
4 Only a ____________ wants to go.	Nur eine **Minderheit** will dahin.
5 He ______________ me that he was right.	Er **überredete** mich, dass er Recht hatte.
6 He _________ _______ _________ _____ the mistake.	Er **nahm** den Fehler **nicht zur Kenntnis**.
7 I _______ his _____________ to an old picture.	Ich **lenkte** seine **Aufmerksamkeit** auf ein altes Bild.
8 I laughed to ________ his ______________.	Ich lachte, um seine **Aufmerksamkeit** zu **erregen**.
9 I can't ______ _____________ when I'm bored.	Ich kann nicht **aufpassen**, wenn ich mich langweile.
10 We've had a few ________ of cheating recently.	Wir hatten in letzter Zeit ein paar **Fälle** von Betrug.
11 The programme was ______________ in 40 countries.	Das Sendung wurde in 40 Ländern **ausgestrahlt**.
12 Grandpa doesn't understand the _____ of computers.	Opa versteht das **Nutzen** von Computern nicht.

20 More about activism

Put the parts in the correct order. The first one has been done for you.

a Activism is not new, but the form it takes has changed a lot over the

b society and the way we live. Forms of activism include writing

c and strike are further examples. Environmental activists want to protect the earth and natural

d change of some type, and is based on the intention to make improvements in

e letters or emails to newspapers or to people in positions of power such

f years. Basically, activism refers to efforts to promote or prevent or

g resources and are often against building new roads or the cutting down of the rainforest.

h as senators, MPs and even the PM, for example, and also launching political

i influence social, political, economic, and more recently also environmental

j to boycott a business. Street marches, public protests, sit-ins in public buildings

k campaigns. Economic activism can include taking actions such as deciding

Answer: a ☐ ☐ ☐ ☐ ☐ ☐ ☐ ☐ ☐ ☐

21 Words and phrases ➜ *(p. 98)*

1 I've got ________ ____ things to do today.	Ich habe heute **eine Menge** zu tun.
2 She's rich. She isn't happy ________.	Sie ist reich. Sie ist **aber** nicht glücklich.
3 She has the ________ to make people laugh.	Sie hat die **Fähigkeit**, Leute zum Lachen zu bringen.
4 The life of ________ ________ must be hard.	Das Leben eines **Nomadenvolkes** muss schwer sein.
5 Have you been a ________ of violence?	Warst du jemals **Opfer** von Gewalt?
6 ________ made him leave his country.	**Verfolgung** brachte ihn dazu, sein Land zu verlassen.
7 This was my very first ________.	Das war mein allererster **Versuch**.
8 He ________ further discussion of the topic.	Er **verbat** eine weitere Diskussion des Themas.

22 Keywords

Rewrite the sentences using the keywords so they mean the same as the original. Don't change the keyword in any way.

1 They both said they had not been in the area. **having**

Both of them ________________________________ been in the area.

2 You're not allowed to smoke anywhere in this building. **forbidden**

Smoking in this building ________________________________.

3 I love it here because there is so much to see and do. **loads**

There are ________________________________ to see and do here, which is why I love it.

4 It's important to listen to the teacher during lessons. **attention**

You have to ________________________________ in class

5 I didn't want to apply for the job, but my mother made me change my mind. **to**

My mother ________________________________ apply for the job.

6 I got up as soon as it was light because I had so much to do. **at**

Because I had so much to do, I got up ________________________________.

7 It's a real pity I didn't buy tickets for their last concert. **not**

I really ________________________________ tickets for their last concert.

8 You'll hurt yourself if you're not careful. **accident**

Be careful, you might ________________________________.

23 Words and phrases ➜ *(pp. 98–101)*

1 Millions died during the ____________.	Millionen sind während des **Holocaust** gestorben.
2 My idea has ______________ support.	Meine Idee hat **weitverbreitete** Unterstützung.
3 He has no ____________ of leaving today.	Er hat keine **Absicht**, heute loszufahren.
4 You just need to ________ some of your ideas.	Du musst einfach einige deiner Ideen **verfeinern**.
5 I'll try to _____________ the main points.	Ich versuche, die Hauptargumente **zusammenzufassen**.
6 She gave me a ___________ of the book.	Sie gab mir eine **Zusammenfassung** des Buches.
7 Do you have any ________ ____ global warming?	Hast du **Beweise für** die Erderwärmung?
8 These are all fields where we grow ______.	Das sind alle Felder, wo wir **Getreide** anbauen.
9 The most important ______ in Asia is rice.	Die wichtigste **Nutzpflanze** in Asien ist Reis.

24 Missing!

Add the missing words to two of the three gaps in each line.

1 My first attempt ________ write a summary was not ________ great so I tried to refine ________ a little.

2 Nomadic ________ people have been victims ________ persecution ________ the 13th century in Europe.

3 Equality means that ________ women want the same pay ________ men ________ the same work.

4 Writing ________ good summaries needs an ability ________ focus ________ the most important points of a text.

5 There are loads ________ reasons why I wanted to persuade you ________ join ________ the march with us.

6 When the waiter came I made an attempt ________ catch ________ attention but he didn't notice ________ me.

7 There have been ________ several cases ________ violence ________ immigrants in the news recently.

8 To get the support ________ young people, the use ________ social media is ________ essential.

9 It's wrong to discriminate ________ people because of their gender, ________ colour, race ________ religion.

10 Activists are ________ people who get involved ________ things; they are not afraid to ________ action.

11 I really didn't feel ________ seeing the film, but it was ________ good ________.

12 I can hear you clearly. ________ line is good, so there's ________ no need to raise ________ voice.

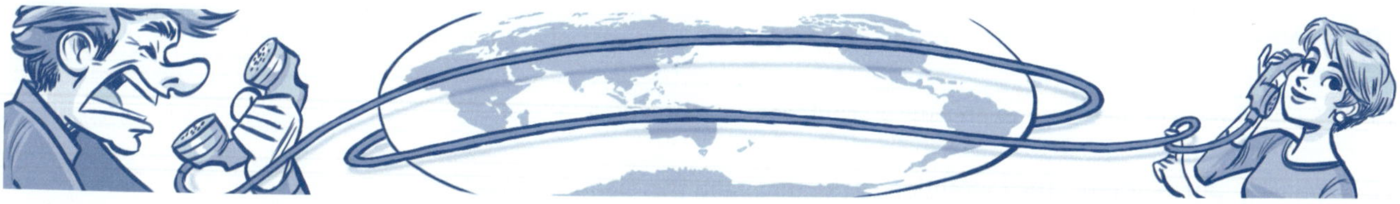

25 Words and phrases → (p. 51)

1 This huge garden is exactly ____ ________.	Dieser Riesengarten hat genau **4,85623 Hektar**.
2 It has been very warm ____________.	**In letzter Zeit** war es sehr warm.
3 The film began with a ____________ picture.	Der Film begann mit einem **schockierenden** Bild.
4 What do you ____________ as a solution?	Was **schlägst** du als Lösung **vor**?
5 We are all looking for a way ____________.	Wir suchen alle nach einem Weg **nach vorne**.
6 What will life be like 50 years________ ______?	Wie wird das Leben **in** 50 Jahren sein?
7 This was a very ______________ scene of the film.	Das war eine sehr **unvergessliche** Szene im Films.
8 My mum __________ ________ bad headaches.	Meine Mutter **leidet an** starken Kopfschmerzen.

26 The right word

Circle the correct word to complete the sentences.

1 It was a really **memorable** • **memory** • **memorial** weekend.

2 If you're ill, don't **suffered** • **suffer** • **suffering** in silence. Say something.

3 I found the news from the war zone really **shocked** • **shock** • **shocking** .

4 I don't really agree with his **summarize** • **summary** • **summery** of events.

5 We discussed the problem and would like to **propose** • **project** • **protest** a solution.

6 There are five **crops** • **acres** • **corn** of **crops** • **acres** on this farm.

7 Her **ability** • **able** • **ableness** to remember lots of detail is very impressive.

8 The writer has **widespreading** • **widely spread** • **widespread** popularity.

9 He made a good **trial** • **attempt** • **go** to make his presentation different from the others.

10 The government wants to **put** • **pass** • **provide** a law against discrimination.

11 The police were in the street to prevent a **civil war** • **Holocaust** • **riot** .

12 I **paid** • **put** • **drew** their attention to the time, and the meeting ended.